Leading Secondary English

Leading Secondary English

Unlock the secrets to building an exceptional English department

Donal Hale

BLOOMSBURY EDUCATION
LONDON OXFORD NEW YORK NEW DELHI SYDNEY

BLOOMSBURY EDUCATION
Bloomsbury Publishing Plc
50 Bedford Square, London WC1B 3DP, UK
Bloomsbury Publishing Ireland Limited
29 Earlsfort Terrace, Dublin 2, D02 AY28, Ireland

BLOOMSBURY, BLOOMSBURY EDUCATION and the Diana logo are
trademarks of Bloomsbury Publishing Plc

First published in Great Britain 2026 by Bloomsbury Publishing Plc
This edition published in Great Britain 2026 by Bloomsbury Publishing Plc

Text copyright © Donal Hale, 2026

Donal Hale has asserted his right under the Copyright, Designs and Patents
Act, 1988, to be identified as Author of this work.

All rights reserved. No part of this publication may be: i) reproduced or
transmitted in any form, electronic or mechanical, including photocopying,
recording or by means of any information storage or retrieval system without
prior permission in writing from the publishers; or ii) used or reproduced in
any way for the training, development or operation of artificial intelligence
(AI) technologies, including generative AI technologies. The rights holders
expressly reserve this publication from the text and data mining exception as
per Article 4(3) of the Digital Single Market Directive (EU) 2019/790

A catalogue record for this book is available from the British Library

ISBN: PB: 978-1-80199-685-3; ePub: 978-1-80199-687-7

2 4 6 8 10 9 7 5 3 (paperback)

Cover design by James Fraser

Typeset by NewGen KnowledgeWorks Pvt. Ltd., Chennai, India
Printed and bound in Great Britain by TJ Books, Padstow, Cornwall

To find out more about our authors and books visit www.bloomsbury.com
and sign up for our newsletters

For product safety related questions contact productsafety@bloomsbury.com

To all the English teachers – the magic weavers –

who shape lives every day.

Contents

Acknowledgements viii

Introduction 1

Part one: Building a culture of excellence

1. Building culture: Destination story and mental models 5
2. The laws: Habits and routines in the classroom 25
3. Upholding the law 55

Part two: Curriculum, pedagogy and assessment

4. Spiral curriculum and schema-building 77
5. Implementing a knowledge-rich curriculum 99
6. Subject-specific pedagogy 117
7. Assessing using curriculum-related expectations 145

Part three: The nuts and bolts of leadership

8. Leading department meetings 173
9. Subject knowledge and expertise 195
10. Lightening the workload for your team 215

Final thoughts: Empowering your leadership and teaching practice 237

Bibliography 239
Index 243

Acknowledgements

Writing this book has been a joy and a privilege, but it was only made possible by others in my life who gave me the confidence to put my ideas out there – even when I felt lacking!

I want to begin by thanking my wonderful wife, Fi. Her unwavering support, even when imposter syndrome would kick in, kept me going throughout the process. I could simply not have done this without her.

It is important to note the extensive influence that working at Trinity Academy Leeds has had on the contents of these pages. I want to thank both Kat Cafferky, my principal, who has always been my champion, and Hannah Collins, our vice principal, who has expertly supported me as curriculum leader of English at TAL. I also want to offer a special thanks to our English department – the finest group of colleagues that I have had the pleasure of working with and leading these last few years.

For those who have contributed case studies for this book – James Dyke, Shabnam Ahmed, Amy Staniforth, Grace Johnston, Kirsty Pole, Elaine McNally, Miriam Hussain and Heather Wright – I will be eternally grateful. Your contributions are truly inspiring and greatly appreciated.

Finally, thank you to the team at Bloomsbury Education (Lucy Tipton, Grace Kelly), who worked tirelessly to ensure that *Leading Secondary English* became a reality – and making a dream of mine come true.

Introduction

Leading an English department in a secondary school is one of the most challenging and most rewarding things that one can do in the education sector.

It is particularly stressful in a landscape where outcomes at Key Stage 4 (Progress 8 or five A*–Cs, including English and maths) drive a significant portion of the whole-school performance measure. However, for many English teachers, the opportunity to design a curriculum and steer pedagogy centred on the power of language and literature makes this a worthwhile trade-off. It certainly is for me.

So, to rebut my opening paragraph somewhat… leading English in a secondary school is an utter privilege.

Yet I do not recall at any point attending a single training session that focused on how to lead an English department effectively – or, at least, training that covered *everything* encompassed in such a role, which is so varied and complex.

Most often, colleagues are promoted from teacher to second-in-department to head of English through the passage of time, accruing experience but with very little bespoke CPD (continuing professional development) on how to do the leadership aspect of the job very well – which is strange, considering that is what you are ultimately paid for in such a role.

This book is my attempt to offer a blueprint – a toolkit, a roadmap (insert your own metaphor here) – for leading the many facets of a secondary school English team. It will not cover everything, but its breadth should help with many aspects of the job role.

It is also incredibly important to note that this blueprint has not been created purely from what I have done as an individual. Fifteen years of teaching in various schools has meant that I have learned from phenomenal leaders, and some of what I include here stems from their work. No one individual has all the answers, and much of what is conceived in this book is inspired by the excellence of others.

The book is broken up into three sections to guide you through the over-arching elements of the job role that I believe are absolutely vital for success:

1. Building a culture of excellence
2. Curriculum, pedagogy and assessment
3. The nuts and bolts of leadership.

You might not agree with all my approaches, but it will allow you to think deeply about leading a team. Indeed, if all this book does is help you to refine your thinking concerning leading English, then I will take that as a win.

To further exemplify the widest range of views, approaches and strategies to best diversify the voices on leadership in secondary English, there are also numerous case studies from fellow leaders linked to the content of some of the chapters within the book. Hopefully, this will add to the breadth of experience that is required for this to be an authentic guidebook for leading secondary English.

Part one

Building a culture of excellence

Chapter 1
Building culture: Destination story and mental models

This chapter covers:

- capturing your English team's shared values and how this shapes culture
- setting a department vision
- the balance between enabling autonomy and ensuring consistency as a leader.

When you speak with any successful leader in education, they will credit building the 'right' culture as the single most important contributor to running a well-oiled and slick organisation. But before we even begin to contemplate what the 'right' culture might be, it is useful to define culture itself to avoid this becoming some buzzword with no depth of meaning.

Culture comes from the Latin word *cultura*, which means growing or cultivation. As a leader, this is what you must do. Your success as a team lives – or dies – by your ability (or inability) to enable each of the beliefs stated below to be the reality for the team that you lead. Here is how I will define culture for the purpose of this book and within the narrow confines of leading a department in a secondary school setting:

Culture is the beliefs held, evidenced by the habits and rituals enacted, leading to a set of behaviours within a secondary English department.

Let us break down the three aspects to building culture and examine them in depth. This is important. Everything that follows in this book springboards from developing an effective culture for a secondary English department.

The beliefs held

This is the foundation to building culture but it often becomes words and not actions, so it is vital to be a little cautious here.

For example, I have never spoken to a leader of an English department who did not say that they had high expectations of their students. This rhetoric, however, is not always matched to reality. Why? Often it is because the habits and rituals – a department's modus operandi – are not consistently applied across all members of a team, and therefore a culture of high expectations has not been realised.

So, whilst it is important to ensure that you can clearly communicate the culture that you are building in your team, always remember: this needs to be self-evident when one watches your team in action.

Before we get there, though, consider what culture you want to create for your department very carefully. For me, the highest-performing English teams that I have worked in, led or observed in action all had the following beliefs that underlined their department's culture:

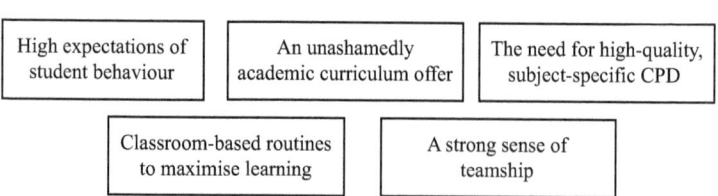

FIGURE 1: Department priorities

I have grouped these beliefs in this way, with no hierarchical ranking, but I would argue that unless student behaviour is excellent, you are hampering your ability to lead an expert English department, even if all the other beliefs are realised.

As a leader of an English department, therefore, you are its cultural architect. You embody the beliefs held, but you also perfectly exemplify the habits and rituals enacted and you establish the behaviours of your team becoming normalised under your charge.

It is also important to remember that culture is more than individual teachers working in isolation. Culture is every teacher expecting the same and working together. Culture is consistency.

Destination story

One method of setting a clear vision for your department – and a very useful thought experiment – is using a *destination story*. In essence, this is the outcome – the external reality – of what you think of when you imagine your team working at its peak functioning capacity. The length of time to reach this 'destination' will vary, depending on a variety of factors, including the maturity of you as a leader and/or of the team that you are leading. Like approaching curriculum design (see Chapter 4), when approaching the beliefs held by your English department, it is useful to consider your endpoint first and work your way backwards.

Setting a realistic time-frame for this to be realised is important. It is unlikely to be achieved in a single academic year; rather, it may be a longer-term aim. This needs to be a minimum of three years to allow implementation to be realised and to see the impact of your leadership.

For example, I wrote the following destination story in May 2023, when working as curriculum leader for English at Trinity Academy Leeds, with a goal of September 2027 for this to be fully embedded as a normal working practice – our modus operandi. This must be ambitious, too. When you do this, you may feel a little awkward, particularly if you are prone to self-deprecation. This is not the time to be humble. This is *your* vision and it should be audacious. If not, how will you push yourself and your team to excellence?

Note: Some of the language may feel alien, but it is part of our shared professional language (and thus very context-specific, as it should be). Later in this chapter, we examine the role of communal language as a means of reinforcing culture. Being able to unpick the destination story is important and necessary along the way.

Notice how the language below mirrors the five beliefs mentioned earlier. I have highlighted the parts in **bold** to show the connection.

Team English: Destination story

The English team are passionate subject experts. We delve into the minutiae – the nuts and bolts and intricacies of both language and literature. ***We draw from evidence-informed practice and the best bets from research to inform our pedagogy****.*

*We offer **an unashamedly knowledge-rich, academic curriculum** that empowers all students to find their voice as great writers and as true literary scholars. Everything in our curriculum is intentional – we use a spiral model to revisit disciplinary knowledge and build students' schemas with concepts that underpin major literary themes. Every member of the team, without exception, knows both the how and the why of what we offer to our students.*

Teaching and learning are exceptional. We are the envy of others across the land. Our reputation precedes us on the national stage. ***Our relentless drive to sweat the small stuff in our habits and routines – but also our subject-specific pedagogy, consistently applied – means that every student gets a world-class English teacher****. This makes successful inevitable; this puts our results in line with the top-performing schools in the country.*

When you enter our corridor, Culture 20 sings to the highest heaven. ***Low-level disruption does not occur; student behaviour is exemplary. We are the mental model to others in the academy: visitors are often led to us first –*** *and are, rightly, blown away by what they witness.*

We support each other. Always. It is side before self, every time.

I can safely say that the above is the culture that I want to build in my department. When this manifests beyond any qualification, I know that we have instilled a culture of excellence. However, that is not to say that improvements – or course corrections – are not required at times too.

Reflection is key. For instance, the following questions are ones that I frequently ask myself to track how successfully we are making inroads to this ultimate destination.

- Is every member of the team able to articulate the 'how and why' of our curriculum offer?
- Is our 'subject-specific pedagogy consistently applied' by every member of the team?
- Are our results 'in line with the top-performing schools in the country'? If not, what needs to change?
- If I ask the principal, would they agree that 'we are the mental model to others in the academy'?

Each of the above needs a careful interrogation using a simple framework: *if* not, *why* not?

Our role as leaders of an English department is to provide the support and challenge where performance is not matching expectations, as established through the destination story.

Mental models

Put simply, a mental model is *an explanation of how something works*. We all have mental models for all we do in teaching and leadership, and they can vary wildly. The point, though, is this: as a leader, you establish the mental models within your department, and you and your team always need to hold yourselves accountable for these.

I use the phrase 'mental model' a lot. It might not be your preferred language. It might feel overtly corporate or dripping with pretension. You do not need to use the phrase if you prefer not to.

However, what it is and how you use this as leader of an English department is vital.

Mental models work best with scripting, or model examples, to support how you want something to be done. They can be used – and indeed are perhaps best used – for minutiae. I firmly believe that you need to sweat the small stuff to develop an expert English department.

How you choose to use mental models to support and develop your team will be based on a variety of factors, including the needs of staff and students, the maturity of your team and what you as a leader consider to require a high degree of consistency across your team.

Much of Chapter 2 is also focused on using mental models to ensure that your team implements department-wide routines and habits in your pursuit of developing an ethic of excellence.

But at this stage, I want to offer a more detailed explanation of how mental models help to shape the five beliefs that underpin an expert English department, as stated earlier in this chapter.

High expectations of student behaviour

As a leader, every student participating in an English lesson in your school should be learning in a classroom with excellent behaviour. Your job is to ensure that this happens for every single member of your team. If there is one weak link here, your culture will erode rapidly.

To clarify, though, the weak link is not a human. Behaviour management requires a clear and robust system that needs to be followed by teachers. Your school might already have a phenomenal behaviour system in place, or this may be absent in your context. Either way, the consistent application of a behaviour system by all members of your team is the goal here.

Most of you will operate a *VCR behaviour system*, which broadly works like this:

- Verbal warning
- Consequence (point on a management information system/detention/move to different seat)
- Removal (with further consequences).

There are thousands of variations of the above across every school in the UK but, generally, behaviour systems work best if there is an opportunity for students to correct their behaviour independently and, failing this, the behaviour results in a sanction. Obviously, the degree of sanctions will also vary from school to school.

I am not going to advise you about what your behaviour management system *should* be. Many of you are subject to a whole-school system, which is absolutely fine. However, what I do want you to think about is your mental model of how each step in a VCR system works in your department and whether all members of your team want the same mental model too.

Verbal warning

With warnings, the pitfalls that I see most commonly are:

- staff being unaware of what behaviour constitutes a verbal warning
- staff issuing a warning (or pre-warning) before the official verbal warning
- staff lacking the knowledge and skill of how best to issue a verbal warning.

Your mental model for your team needs to ensure that these are avoided in order to make sure that any first step in behaviour management is consistently applied.

Staff's lack of awareness of what behaviour constitutes a verbal warning is often because schools and departments don't consider the range of scenarios that are likely to occur in the classroom to which the behaviour policy will be applied. For me, this is the best way to show staff how the behaviour system actually works in practice.

One way to tackle this is to ask all staff in your team to write down all the scenarios in which they have issued a verbal warning (or where they envisage that they would need to issue one) and explore this collectively as a team. Here, you can flush out where the inevitable inconsistencies lie within your team.

Examples of where there has been debate about verbal warning issues in my current department include:

- A student makes eye contact (non-verbal communication) with another student during teacher input.
- A student continues to write after the teacher asks for pens down.
- A student fails to speak when instructed to start a 'turn and talk' (a structured discussion in pairs).
- A student puts their hand up when you have instructed the class to keep hands down during independent practice.
- A student does not begin their 'do now' (or first task upon entering the classroom) promptly having entered the classroom.

I focused on less obvious examples of poor behaviour here to illustrate the need for consistency of behaviour management at a 'sweating the small stuff' level.

It is this approach to behaviour more generally that is likely to lead to a culture of high expectations.

Imagine, then, that you have one teacher in your department who does *not* issue a verbal warning when a student fails to speak during 'turn and talk' and the rest of the team does. You, as a leader, believe that you have high expectations for student behaviour, but the student who does not get a warning for failing to engage in 'turn and talk' suddenly has lower expectations of them than other students in that same school.

Whilst this seems rather small-scale, imagine if you have several teachers who do not give a verbal warning for *all* the scenarios mentioned above, even if they do in some of them. Inconsistency – this affects students' behaviour, as it will lead to a belief from them that they have different expectations from different English teachers. If you pick up the same student who was never sanctioned for refusing to engage in 'turn and talk' in later years at school, suddenly conflict arises because they can (rightly) claim that this was not an issue elsewhere.

As part of your leadership of the department, you ultimately decide whether a verbal warning is appropriate for any classroom scenario, and your team must act as you do. Your mental model must be their mental model to ensure a parity of experience from students in all classrooms of your corridor.

Similar to this, you need to ensure that all of your team only ever give one warning before escalation through the behaviour system. This is a huge bugbear for me: the warning(s) that precede *the warning*. A warning is just that, but here is an example of a terrible enaction of high expectations and the use of verbal warning that I have overheard in a school:

> *Stop that NOW! If you continue to disrupt the lesson like this, that will be your C1!*

For context, C1 was the school's code for a verbal warning. The imperative to stop arose from a student throwing a pen at another student. Notice, though, how verbal warnings had clearly been issued prior to the official warning. This undermines the entire behaviour system because, essentially, the teacher is enacting the belief that 'I can offer warnings prior to a real warning'. Again, a warning is a warning. Any ambiguity here leads to an erosion of any culture that you are trying to build around student behaviour.

This example above also illustrates the importance of ensuring that your team has the knowledge and skill to issue a verbal warning effectively. My mental model for issuing a verbal warning is that it must be delivered firmly, and in a calm and professional tone.

Scripting examples and demonstrating them (either through lesson observations or in deliberate practice) will increase the likelihood of your mental model being lived out in the classrooms of your team.

> *Max, that is your C1. We do not make eye contact with others during my input, thank you.*
>
> *Issy, I am going to give you a C1 as a reminder to put pens down when instructed first time.*
>
> *Abdul, this is a C1, I want to hear your fantastic ideas in our 'turn and talk'.*
>
> *Mina, C1. Hands remain down during independent practice. Thank you.*
>
> *Sami, I know you get to work quicker than that to begin Recall 6. C1.*

All of the above also narrate the 'why' of staff issuing a verbal warning, to make this clear to students and reduce any fight-back. Trust me – if you do this relentlessly for micro-behaviours, you are far less likely to have to deal with bigger issues.

Consequence

It would be wonderful if teenagers always heeded a teacher's warning and no escalation of a behaviour system was required, but this is not the reality of the job. In fact, as an English team, your staff are likely to see students three, four or maybe five times per week, so inevitably students will push the boundaries beyond the verbal warning.

When this happens, the principles as outlined with verbal warning strategies are the exact same. Consistency is key. However, at this stage, because managing the behaviour is perceived as higher stakes than a warning, staff often do wobble a little.

My approach is: if a student has not met a teacher's expectations for the *second* time in a lesson, there must a consequence or sanction for this. It is a numbers game, really. The first time a student does not behave, the warning is a final opportunity for them to modify their behaviour before escalation occurs.

As a leader, you need to make sure that this really does happen, in every interaction with every member of the English department in every lesson.

Imagine the two scenarios below. In the first scenario, one member of the English department (Mr Allen) fails to issue a consequence (C2) for a student calling out, having already issued a verbal warning (C1). In the second scenario, another member of the same department (Ms Davis) issues a consequence for the same behaviour from a student in her class.

Scenario 1

Mr Allen: *In a moment, I am going to ask someone to answer a question. Hands remain down. We do not call out, even if we know the answer. What does Dickens compare Scrooge's solitary nature to in St—*
Emma: *It's an oyster, sir! 'Solitary as an oyster'.*
Mr Allen: *That's right, Emma. But please do not call out the answer.*

Scenario 2

Ms Davis: *Remember, everyone, hands down, no shouting out. What does Dickens compare Scrooge's solitary nature to in St—*
Simon: *Oh Miss, Miss! He uses a metaphor – 'solitary as an oyster'.*
Ms Davis: *Whilst correct, Simon, that is your C2. We do not call out. Thank you.*

You could imagine how each of the above might happen with different teachers in your team, but clearly Ms Davis has higher expectations of her students than Mr Allen does of his. Ms Davis issues a sanction after establishing the means of participation, whereas Mr Allen merely requests his student (Emma) not to call out. If culture is consistency, can you truly have a culture of high expectations in your department if Emma gets away with breaking a classroom rule and Simon does not? The answer is 'no'.

What is frustrating about Mr Allen is that he set the high expectations prior to posing his question, yet did not uphold them by consistently applying the behaviour system. His mental model is different from that of Ms Davis, and most likely from yours as a leader, and therefore needs to be addressed urgently before the culture is diluted.

Removal from class

I want to add to Scenario 2 with Ms Davis to stress-test how high your expectations for student behaviour as a leader should stretch. Below is my mental model for escalating further if the following secondary behaviour were to occur following the issue of a consequence.

> Ms Davis: *Remember, everyone, hands down, no shouting out. What does Dickens compare Scrooge's solitary nature to in St—*
>
> Simon: *Oh Miss, Miss! He uses a metaphor – 'solitary as an oyster'.*
>
> Ms Davis: *Whilst correct, Simon, that is your C2. We do not call out. Thank you.*
>
> Simon: [mumbling] *Yeah, but it was right…*
>
> Ms Davis: *Simon, C3. We do not argue back. Thank you.*

Previously, you may have been advised to ignore secondary behaviours. Arguably, the mumbling is a direct result of the C2 being issued, so escalating further is not necessary. I disagree. We only hold students to the highest of expectations if we are willing to explain (and sanction accordingly) each moment where expectations are not met. Again, it is a numbers game. By this point of the lesson, Simon has not met expectations *three* times; therefore, a C3 (classroom removal) is logical and appropriate.

Once more, if this is *your* mental model, you need to ensure that staff hold students to the same level of accountability. Teachers that I have led have struggled with this; your job is to support them, reassure them and, ultimately, ensure that this becomes habitual in their practice too if you truly want a culture of high expectations.

The moment at which a member of your team thinks that they will be harangued by you for doing so, this all falls apart. Make sure that it is crystal clear and always do what you say that you do.

An unashamedly academic curriculum offer

I attended a very high-performing grammar school in Northern Ireland. I am not suggesting that the grammar system is one that we should adopt elsewhere. The reason why I mention it, however, is that I have always associated school with rigour and academia. Whilst the arts are incredibly important and I value them highly in a whole-school context, when leading an English curriculum, this needs to have a sharp academic focus.

When I first trained in 2009, English was not considered by many an academic subject in the traditional sense. Often, notions of disciplinary knowledge were ignored in favour of a skills-based approach. This led to a genericism of the subject (and, consequently, the pedagogy that underpinned delivering this subject), which did a disservice to English.

For example, viewing English as a vehicle to develop skills of comprehension, inference and evaluation often meant that English curricula lacked any substance. It meant that studying literature was not rooted in the knowledge that one should possess about literature, but in a superficial and surface-level approach to teaching English. It is no wonder that many departments (including my own when I first started teaching) saw PEE (Point, Evidence, Explanation) or PEA (Point, Evidence, Analysis) as the panacea for students doing well in English.

If you do not quite understand what that has meant in practice, consider this: in the English secondary National Curriculum between 2007 and 2013, not a single literary text was named. No specific component of grammar was mentioned. It was utterly devoid of any factual knowledge that students were expected to acquire. In fact, there was just one paragraph of suggested authors for the tens of pages of skills specifications that preceded it.

The current English secondary National Curriculum, first introduced in September 2014, is even fewer pages. In fact, it is remarkably brief and specifies even fewer authors: Shakespeare is the only explicitly named author, and not a single novel, play or poem is mentioned. So even though many are weary of the rise of the knowledge-rich curriculum in England, our National Curriculum is, in fact, a curriculum absent of any specific literary texts.

What this leads to is the opposite to the mental model that I hold (and want my team to hold) about our English curriculum. Students do not really need to *know* the texts that they study; rather, they should apply their skills to *any* text. The idea of transferrable skills in the absence of students having foundational knowledge in English dilutes the power of our subject.

Chapter 7 considers how this dilution was (and arguably still is) caused by assessment practices in English, but for now I want to focus on developing a mental model that reflects the content of an academic, knowledge-rich approach to an English curriculum.

Please do not misunderstand me: a knowledge-rich approach to an English curriculum does not eradicate skills. In fact, skills, I would argue, are merely a kind of knowledge. More specifically, skills stem from a knowledge of *how* to do something. Often, knowledge is needed to then carry out a skill. The issue with a skills-based approach in previous curriculum iterations was the absence of seeing knowledge as a prerequisite to carrying out a skill in English.

It is probably best to demonstrate what I mean by this with a specific example. Many of you will have taught – or currently teach – *Animal Farm* by George Orwell. You could absolutely teach this novel to support students to develop 'skills' in literary analysis without teaching knowledge of fables, anthropomorphism, allegory, satire or the Russian Revolution. However, to do so means that students do not really know the text. It is merely the vehicle at the behest of skills.

Let us imagine that you are looking at *Animal Farm* and you are teaching a class about the character of Napoleon. When first introduced to us, he is described as follows:

> 'Napoleon was a large, rather fierce-looking Berkshire boar, the only Berkshire on the farm, not much of a talker, but with a reputation for getting his own way. (Orwell, 1945).'

We could teach students to analyse language at word level (perhaps because this is what is required for GCSE English language), and so you might ask questions such as:

- What does the phrase 'fierce-looking' imply about Napoleon's character?
- If Napoleon is 'not much of a talker', what does this suggest about his character?
- What does Orwell mean when he says that Napoleon has a 'reputation for getting his own way'?

There is nothing wrong with these questions in and of themselves. What's missing in a skills-based approach is the knowledge that students must possess (and be explicitly taught) in order to truly understand Orwell's work.

Here is the 'knowledge' that students require to write a character analysis of Orwell's Napoleon:

- Students must have a secure knowledge of the plot of *Animal Farm* and, know about Napoleon's arc within the novel. Otherwise, students cannot make connections between his physical appearance ('fierce-looking') and his fierce nature (for example, his callous treatment of Boxer).
- Students must understand anthropomorphism. 'Berkshire' is referenced twice, so students need to know that he is a pig but actually has human attributes.
- From this, students must comprehend that the novel is an allegory. Napoleon represents something (corrupt leaders) or, more specifically, someone (Joseph Stalin). Knowledge of Stalinist Russia allows students to truly understand what Orwell means when he states that Napoleon gets 'his own way'.
- Knowledge of how fables and satire work may then allow students to articulate authorial intent (for example, Orwell is satirising the hypocrisy of a supposed-communist state led by a dictator).

There may be even more essential knowledge than I have stated here. The point is this: knowledge will allow students to apply the skill of writing about character in a much more meaningful way. Again, it is why GCSE English language papers where students write about unseen literature can often offer simplistic responses that value skills (I mean – look at the mark schemes) over secure knowledge of a literary text.

You might have your own views about this, and they will invariably affect and shape your mental model. For me, an academic curriculum does not shy away from teaching students about the disciplinary knowledge underpinning my *Animal Farm* example. In fact, as you will read in Chapter 5, it shapes curriculum design.

The need for high-quality, subject-specific CPD

As the leader of an English department, you will likely have the sole responsibility for ensuring that your team receives high-quality, subject-specific CPD, although many of you have probably felt that not enough time (and therefore value) is given to this.

This is not surprising when you consider the national context. According to the Teaching and Learning International Survey, just under 50 per cent of teachers in England had done some curriculum-related CPD in the previous year, compared with 80 per cent in Singapore and 90 per cent in Shanghai (Jerrim and Sims, 2019).

I tell you this with envy when I say that we are miles apart in this area – especially when you also consider that in Singapore, 100 hours per year are made available to teachers for CPD (Schleicher, 2018).

You will not have 100 hours with your team, so the time that you do have needs to be utilised well. There will be more detail in Chapter 8 about ensuring that department meeting time is not used ineffectually, so that time for CPD is protected and treated as sacrosanct.

Chapter 6 will also offer much detail on how to develop a culture of subject-specific CPD. At this stage for your mental model, it is more of a psychological battle. As a leader, you need to prioritise this to ensure that your team reaps its benefits.

Classroom-based routines to maximise learning

As a leader, you cannot be in every classroom along your corridor at every moment because, of course, you will often be in your own classroom. The chances are that you will have established some excellent classroom-based routines for *your* students. But do all the teachers in your team do the same? How do you know?

Consistency with classroom-based routines forms much of Chapters 2 and 3, but I want to offer a mental model that is the goal of enacting those routines. For me, I am unapologetic about what we should offer to the parents of students under our charge: a return on investment. This might sound a little cold or clinical, but what I mean is that our job is to teach English for the allocated time during which we have students in our timetables, and I do not believe that any time should be wasted in doing so. Without sounding overly dramatic, every moment counts.

This is never truer than for those of you working in schools with high numbers of disadvantaged students. I have worked in such schools throughout much of my career and I have witnessed first-hand the importance of not wasting time in the classroom to ensure better outcomes for the most vulnerable students.

Here is the goal that I tell my team we should all be aiming for:

From entering your classroom to exiting your classroom, no learning time should be wasted. The use of our routines will ensure that students are focused and on-task and each routine that you lead is done quickly and slickly to ensure that time is spent on maximising the learning of our students.

I appreciate that this sounds lofty. The routines that are used in pursuit of this goal are fully explained in the subsequent chapters.

A strong sense of teamship

A particular phrase from the destination story example earlier truly exemplifies what I mean about building a strong sense of teamship: side before self. This use of shared professional language is key. I use it all the time. For example, when asking my team to ensure that they are always at their classroom door at a lesson transition, I will qualify this with *side before self*.

However, phraseology is not enough on its own. Your team needs to embody this, and in order for that to happen, you need to set the example of what this looks like.

In my experience of working for the leaders of an English department (and I hope that this would be said about me, too), the very best leaders have always put the mission above themselves. This ranges from small things, like carrying resources to a teacher to save them a job, to always ensuring that feedback is delivered in a timely manner following a lesson observation.

Consistency vs autonomy

By now, you will have noticed how often I have used the word *consistency*. This word sometimes gets people's backs up a little.

One criticism of much that I have outlined so far might be that there appears to be a lack of teacher autonomy. I often hear the goal of enabling or achieving autonomy lauded as the pinnacle – the mental model, if you will – of an excellent teacher, department or school.

When I first started my career, I believed that autonomy was the by-product of being an excellent teacher. For instance, after a few years of my career, and having secured a position leading teaching and learning across a school, I started to notice that no one came to observe me teach anymore. I was even relocated to a classroom in an area of the school that most staff did not even know existed!

I would hear staff say – or indeed be told by senior members of staff – that I could be trusted. I did not need to be observed. The students were in safe hands. And other things to this effect.

I was proud. Boastful at times, even. I thought that I had reached the ultimate goal in teaching: I was such a brilliant teacher that I did not need to be managed. I had *autonomy*.

Of course, this was nonsense – in so many ways. But I want to unpick one thing in particular: this might be good for an individual, but it does not help the greater good of both a department and the students within a school.

In other circumstances, I had a member of the team demand autonomy to teach what they wanted, when they wanted, how they wanted. Again, this becomes much more about fuelling the ego of *that* teacher rather than supporting the learning of students in the long term.

So, why do teachers often say that we want greater autonomy? And is this necessarily a good thing?

Well, as you might expect by now, I want to consider its meaning linguistically. Let me indulge in some morphological study:

auto – nomy

Auto comes from the Ancient Greek for 'self'; *nomos* refers to 'law'. One way in which to interpret this is: individuals decide what they do, with the implied lack of accountability that often comes from this.

I want to take a different view. Instead of striving to being self-governed, let us consider the inverse. The laws are the tools that help to govern the self.

With this leaning, one could argue that autonomy, therefore, is really about how the laws (or, in a school context, the policies and procedures) hold you (the *self*) to account.

To build upon this further, my assertion is that you, as the leader of an English department, need to establish these laws. You need to hold yourself, and those you lead, accountable to these laws.

I have never witnessed an excellent English department engage in *lawlessness*.

However, a careful caveat is needed at this point. At no stage in this book will I say that you *must* do what I do. But I will say this: you need to have a clear set of laws by which your team abides if you want to build culture. Consistent upholding of these laws is what will build the culture that you strive to create.

As a starting point, it is useful to think of what these are in broad strokes. For example, the laws that you have for your department might include things like:

- We will always warmly greet students at the door at the beginning of a lesson.
- We will ensure that lessons always begin in silence.

- We will use centralised PowerPoints/booklets/knowledge organisers (summary sheets presenting the core knowledge and contextual facts needed for a topic. For example, key vocabulary, quotes, themes and motifs etc.).

This is far from exhaustive and you might already be screaming in your head: *Yes, but they also need to do THIS, too.*

The next chapter will add more detail to some of the laws by which I would want my team to abide – in other words, the habits and routines of my department that I think are effective in building a culture for excellence.

Some you may agree with wholeheartedly; others you may want to tweak; others you might decide do not fit into the culture that you wish to build for your team. Wherever your thinking on this falls, remember that you are responsible for enacting the laws of your department.

Chapter 2
The laws: Habits and routines in the classroom

This chapter covers:

- the importance of establishing the 'laws' in your department
- the habits and routines that you expect to see in every English classroom, e.g. entry/exit routines, use of mini-whiteboards, cold-calling, etc.
- concrete examples and scripts of what the habits and routines look like in action.

As English teachers, we sometimes tend to get lost in the abstract, the conceptual, the nuance, the exploration of universal human truths. That is fine, and indeed something that makes our day jobs an absolute joy at times.

However, when it comes to ensuring that all students have an excellent climate for learning from all the teachers in your department, it is time to get concrete, practical and, well, boring even.

Adam Boxer, lead practitioner of science at the Totteridge Academy in North London, summarised this well in a tweet a number of years ago:

> 'When it comes to teaching, variety is not the spice of life. Routines, habits and consistency rule the game.' (Boxer, 2021)

I must say that I agree completely. This even became the title of my talk at the inaugural national Litdrive Conference in 2023: 'Routines, habits and consistency across an English department'. And from there, of course, it became the inspiration to write this book!

I realised that it is exactly what I have been telling my ITT (initial teacher training) students this year, to mitigate the fact that they arrive in October and begin teaching without witnessing first-hand the slog that has gone into establishing routines to enable effective behaviour for learning. To their fresh eyes, they often assume that the class is inherently disciplined, focused and respectful to their teacher.

Often, this is just not the case. In fact, I would go as far as to say that no school is lucky enough to have thousands of young people enter their building, with all of them able to self-regulate and manage their learning without routines and habits being explicitly taught by staff.

This chapter outlines the routines that enable habits to form that are consistently followed to build a culture of excellence. You will notice that many of the routines stem from Doug Lemov's *Teach Like a Champion* (2021). I make no apologies for that – it is the ultimate playbook to ensure that you have a calm, orderly climate for learning, which is essential for all that you do as the leader of your English department. However, these have been adapted by me and you will, of course, adapt them to suit your own context further.

1. Meet and greet

I understand that many schools will have school-wide systems that need to be followed. Largely, this massively helps in building a culture of excellence, so many of you reading may be required to do this already. But, if not, my advice as a leader is to ensure that your whole team do this and that you are dogged in your expectations that they do so.

> **Routine:** At every lesson transition, staff stand outside their classroom door ready to meet and greet their students to begin all lessons.

The purpose behind this routine is an important one. It allows staff to build positive relationships with students from the minute they arrive at their lesson. As a leader, you must therefore ensure that all teaching staff are at their classroom door at lesson changeover to positively meet and greet students.

You also need to provide explicit guidance as to how that greeting or interaction should take place. This consistency is vital to make it easier for all staff within your team to have a clear mental model from which to work.

For example, when welcoming a class, insist that all students are greeted by name and with positive/constructive comments as they pass through your door, ready to begin the lesson. How this sounds will vary depending on school context and any shared professional language used across a department and/or school, but the following mini-scripts should give a flavour of how the routine is implemented.

There are two main benefits that come from 'meet and greet' as students cross through a classroom door:

1. Implementing a clear system of how students conduct themselves as they enter each classroom in your department. In essence, students are offered the mental model, regularly and habitually, of how best to enter a classroom ready to learn.
   - *Abdi is walking with pace and purpose down the corridor, ready to begin immediately.*
   - *Sam is already working through her 'do now' in silence, well done Sam.*
   - *Jemima has already started to put pen to paper, one beautiful answer already.*
   - *Emma is ready, first one with pen in hand, equipment all ready.*
2. Strengthening relationships with a warm greeting should not be underestimated. This provides the mental model of how to be polite and respectful to your students.
   - *Great to see you, Jasmine. I'm really looking forward to hearing what you make of Scrooge in our reading today.*

- *I like how quickly you've settled there, Danar, great concentration, lovely extended responses.*
- *Good morning, Luke. I can't wait to see how you are going to build on how brilliantly you did last lesson.*
- *Thank you, Sara; you always get started so promptly and set a brilliant example for others.*

To have the desired impact, this approach should be used by all staff when greeting students outside the classroom and in social areas too, helping students to feel truly seen by their teachers, but also setting the expectation that all interactions are founded on the principles of politeness and respect. This is the baseline for all truly great teaching, and therefore it will maximise students' learning in the longer term too.

2. Silent entry

I may be challenged on this, but I have never, ever observed a calm and purposeful lesson start where students did not enter the classroom in silence. I always advocate for students entering the classroom in my department in absolute silence.

For those reading this who think that this seems a little cold or clinical, remember that this is balanced by the warm greeting that students receive at the door during 'meet and greet' as described previously.

> **Routine:** For every lesson, students enter the classroom in absolute silence and begin the lesson with a focus on learning immediately.

If we are truly going to have high expectations of our students, then we need to be consistent and ensure that the messages that we give our students are crystal clear. Many schools will tell you that they have high expectations of their students, but they often lack the consistency and clarity between classrooms to achieve high expectations.

Language is also important here. Entering a classroom 'calmly' or 'quietly' is too subjective. It will lead to inconsistency in your English corridor. Silence is clean: no debate, no discussion and a clear expectation – and, I would argue, a very reasonable one. Lesson time is finite. We must make the most of all available resources that we have to deliver our curriculum.

As a leader, your job is to make sure that your team achieves this in every classroom, 100 per cent of the time. This means ensuring that your team have you as their mental model of what this looks like and that you will always flag up with staff any instances where this routine does not occur as it should. As stated previously, routines only became true habits if done repeatedly over a significant period of time.

For your students, this also offers a high degree of psychological safety. All my English lessons begin in silence and focus on my learning.

Like 'meet and greet', you want to establish mini-scripts so that your team knows what this sounds and feels like when they implement the routine in their respective classrooms:

1. Implementing a clear system of how students conduct themselves as they begin each lesson in your department. In essence, students are offered the mental model, regularly and habitually, of how to make the most of every moment inside the classroom.
   - *Joshua has arrived in silence and has started his Recall 6 – well done.*
   - *Claudia is already on question 3 – silence is clearly helping you to concentrate.*
   - *Abdullah, you can see everyone in silence. Can I remind you that we do this to ensure that you can concentrate on the Recall 6 questions.*
   - *Thank you, 7E, my last class came in perfectly, I know that you will do the same.*
2. Strengthening relationships where specific and proportionate praise can be offered to students for meeting classroom expectations early in the lesson.
   - *Milan, you came into the room in silence, this is setting a great example.*

- *John, we enter in silence so that you can concentrate fully.*
- *Mya, we enter in silence so that you can get better at recall.*
- *7E, you entered today exactly how I wanted you to. Trust me, this will help with your learning.*

3. Do now/bell task/Recall 6

This is what students do as their first task upon entering the classroom in silence.

This could be a range of things, but my advice is to have the same thing every time. Consistency is important in order to build an effective learning culture. Students value the psychological safety of knowing what to expect in all lesson starts, so this complements 'meet and greet' and 'silent entry' well. These can be adversely affected, though, if there is too much variance to how lessons begin. Keep it simple.

I use a form of recall/retrieval practice as the opener of my lesson, with a simple low-stakes quiz of six questions – hence, Recall 6.

The questions are a mix of content from the last lesson, last week and last term, as appropriate, to build and strengthen students' long-term memory. It might look like this:

1. How did Dickens feel about the vulnerable and disadvantaged in society?
2. What word means 'intending to teach'?
3. What is the enemy of man in 'Exposure'?
4. What does the mother lean on 'like a wishbone' in 'Poppies'?
5. Which poem starts 'Suddenly he awoke and was running'?
6. What is the speaker remembering in the poem 'Remains'?

This ensures that students are focused on learning immediately and it is easy for the teacher to manage – in terms of both behaviour management and workload. Is it a little boring? Yes! Does that matter? Absolutely not.

I used to do more engaging lesson starters earlier in my career. To offer an anecdote from my NQT (newly qualified teacher – the precursor to early career teacher or ECT) year in 2010, the below is what used to shape my lesson starter. I find it rather embarrassing now!

I was teaching students metaphor in the days when Ofsted discourse was about 'engaging' lessons and 'inspiring' students, which (in 2010) meant being FUN.

I focused so much more on exemplifying metaphor through 'cool pop culture references' – for me, this was often song lyrics of bands I liked, and which most of my students couldn't care less about.

If I reflect on something that I taught this year – the use of a conceit in Jason Reynolds' verse novel *Long Way Down* – what I used to do could not be any more different from my teaching approach now.

We teach Year 8s about how Reynolds uses metaphor to compare grief to a tooth being ripped out. The vehicle is such a rich one to examine with students. They love it. They get it! And that's really enough.

However, 2010 me wouldn't have been satisfied with that. I know that I would have done something cringeworthy. What, you ask?

I played Greenday's 'Give me Novocaine' as students entered the room as part of their lesson starter (that might have even just been the starter!). To be fair, there is a similar metaphor ('It's like a throbbing toothache of the mind').

This would have 'hooked' them. It would have been 'inspiring'. But it would have been an utter waste of time.

So I now advise employing starter tasks, based on students' learning and utilising retrieval practice to strengthen long-term memories. This is the business that we are in: making students excellent learners of English and literature.

4. Three, two, one, whiteboards

In a survey conducted by Teacher Tapp in January 2024, just 34 per cent of English teachers claim to use mini-whiteboards (MWBs) regularly in their classroom.

Indeed, MWBs often elicit strong opinions from English teachers, and their use seems to divide our community. We either seem to be die-hard advocates for their use in lessons or we reject them outright. I am in the former camp. However, it must be said that, like any pedagogical tool, it is how they are used that will determine their effectiveness.

To be clear, there are certainly moments to use MWBs in the English classroom and there are also incidences when it is a waste of time.

When I have introduced them into different departments, I have often (but not always!) been given a list of reasons why they are not worth using in the secondary English classroom. In no particular order, they include:

- cost
- behaviour
- time
- lack of permanence
- only useful for factual recall.

I will address each of these in turn, before I explain how I ask my team to use them and the routine that we use to ensure that they are used as effectively as possible in the English classroom.

My questions to the nay-sayers are usually:

- Does another method enable high thinking and participation ratios?
- Does another method allow you to check the understanding of a whole class in a single moment of the lesson?
- Does another method allow for consolidation prior to independent practice as effectively?
- Does another method allow you as teacher to better watch the thinking of students in real time?

The lack of an answer to all these questions has always justified the use of MWBs, despite the potential barriers outlined below, which can be overcome.

Cost

Of course, as heads of department, we are restricted by school budgets. I do not underestimate the challenge of this and it could often be the reason why English departments are unwilling to spend money on the equipment required to effectively use MWBs (pens and erasers are needed too, remember!). However, MWBs need to viewed in terms of their return on investment. When used well, they enhance the teaching and learning of your team, and anything that does so needs to be prioritised in a budget.

Behaviour

I always find this an interesting one. My assertion is that MWBs do not so much *create* bad behaviour as *reveal* it. If MWBs are going to lead to decline in student behaviour, there is often a wider issue with behaviour. If a classroom culture is well established, and if how students use MWBs is explicitly taught and reinforced, then there is no reason why MWBs should act as the vehicle for poor behaviour. If, for example, you have students doodling in an exercise book, the solution is not to stop using pens or exercise books. Like everything in classrooms, there is an element of classroom management required to ensure that MWBs work effectively. I will soon offer my suggestion of a routine that increases the likelihood that poor behaviour does not affect their use.

Time

Time is, of course, precious in teaching. As with the financial costs associated with the use of MWBs, you need to ensure that there is not an opportunity cost in relation to time spent on their usage. Again, there needs to be a return on (time) investment. If you're going to use MWBs, then you really do have to think carefully about where you will store them and how you will get them in front of students and then returned to storage. This needs to be routinised and explicitly taught to students to increase efficiency in their use. All classroom strategies require an investment of time, but MWBs are absolutely worth it.

Lack of permanence

Ah, the classic: if they have not written something down in their exercise books, they have not learned anything. We know that this is simply not true. In fact, when you review a student's book, the learning so often (in hindsight) becomes decontextualised to the point where it is of little use.

For example, let us say that that students are writing down answers to a retrieval question: 1. What does Dickens compare Scrooge's solitary nature to? The chances are that students will have written '1. Oyster'.

Of course, maybe they have written out the question in full as well, but surely that is a much bigger time thief than MWBs?

If the reason why members of your team need students to write everything down is due to fear of SLT (senior leadership team) checking books, then this is a bigger fight that you must have within your school to ensure that you can uphold the laws of your department, as discussed in Chapter 3.

Only useful for factual recall

Like anything in teaching, it is how you use MWBs that matters. Should students draft an essay on mini-whiteboards? No. And whilst the nature of the subject is inherently different from maths and science, there are definitely things that MWBs can be used for in English, such as:

- recall/retrieval of core knowledge (e.g. definition of a simile, an apt quotation, plot details)
- crafting at sentence level (e.g. writing an appositive phrase, thesis statement)
- generating ideas prior to a 'turn and talk' activity (e.g. examples of women's lack of agency in *I am Malala*).

I do not think that we should simply dismiss the scope of their use in English as limited purely because Year 11s write extended essays at GCSE.

Have a clear line with your department as to the rationale of why MWBs are used, and constantly reinforce this message to ensure that the right teaching and learning culture is established and that this does not become a performative tool.

For example:

MWBs are used by the English department frequently in lessons to check for student understanding, to help to structure discussion and to aid quality responses through rehearsal/redrafting of ideas.

As always, if staff understand the why, then they are more likely to do what you want them to do.

> **Routine:** For every use of MWBs in lessons, teachers must follow the system of three, two, one, whiteboards every single time.

So now that you have decided that MWBs are worth using in your department, you need to have a routine in place for their consistent usage to ensure that you maximise their potential in the classroom. I have found that three, two, one, whiteboards is the best system to use.

Below is a mental model that you can share and uphold with all teachers in your team:

- All students show their responses to their teacher in the exact same way, following the command: *three… two… one… whiteboards.*
- After this command is given, students should hold their MWB at chest level. Students at the back should hold it above their head so that every board is easily visible to the teacher.
- Do not be afraid to repeat this instruction as many times as necessary to ensure that all students are clear about expectations.
- When MWBs are used as a method to check understanding, teachers should ensure that this is authentic and that time is spent checking each answer. If a student's answer is correct, the teacher should ask that same student to lower their board and sit in silence, tracking forward.

- Incorrect boards should remain held aloft, and the teacher should select as appropriate to explore any misconceptions with a student or group.
- The teacher may signal to a full class 'whiteboards down' when appropriate.
- All students at all times must be part of this slick routine, and verbally reminded with a verbal warning/behaviour point/appropriate sanction if they fail to meet these expectations.
- This routine ensures that no time is wasted in the lesson and that no students are opting out or off-task.

5. Exit 3

As discussed in 'meet and greet', the starts of lessons help to establish a calm, orderly atmosphere in the classrooms of your department. How a lesson ends – and the routine for this – needs to achieve the same goal.

> **Routine:** All lessons end with the use of Exit 3 to ensure an orderly, silent transition into the English corridor.

There are many different names that you may wish to use for this routine, but I currently use 'Exit 3'. It is clean; there are three things that I expect all students in all classrooms to do at the end of all lessons. Notice my use of 'all' here – consistency, as always, is key.

The script, or PowerPoint template if that is your thing, runs as follows:

1. Pack away equipment in silence.
2. Stand behind your desk in silence.
3. Wait to be dismissed one row at a time.

> *All lessons should be brought to a timely and calm end, ensuring that there is enough time for students to pack away their equipment and stand in silence behind their desks, awaiting their teacher's instructions. Students should not be dismissed until every child is following the routine, with no exceptions. Students should be dismissed quickly and quietly from the classroom to walk silently to their next classroom or social time.*

Not only will you ensure that English lessons end calmly, but you are massively helping students' next teacher, who is more likely to have a calm beginning to *their* lesson because of how the English lessons end.

6. I say, you say

This routine is focused on introducing new vocabulary to students, which, as teachers, we do a lot. It has been suggested that for a new word to truly be learned (and lodged in the long-term memory), students need to be exposed to it at least 17 times in varying contexts of usage.

My go-to for vocabulary instruction is Isabelle Beck, co-author of *Bringing Words to Life* (2013), who argues that to close the often-vast word gap that students possess, new vocabulary must be taught explicitly and in context to students. Previously, I have allowed students to conduct lengthy searches in dictionaries or, worse still, too often allowed students to guess the meaning or definition of a word not previously taught. We must give our students lots of brilliant words to enable them to articulately describe the world around them.

> **Routine:** Teachers should use 'I say, you say' to encourage learners with the correct pronunciation of Tier 2 and 3 words and to give both a clear definition of the word and an example of the word in context.

Disclaimer: You cannot, nor should you, use this routine for every new word that appears in your lesson. Instead, you need to ensure that it is used for high-leverage words within your curriculum mapping. Prior to teaching a unit of work, leaders should identify key vocabulary so that teachers know whether or not to use 'I say, you say' for a particular word choice.

In the script below, there is an example of using 'I say, you say' based on a concept that might recur throughout your curriculum planning.

> Miss Adams: *Victorian Society had a clear power structure, a hierarchy. Hierarchy is an interesting word, as the suffix 'archy' comes from the Greek for 'rule'. Hierarchy, then, is a clear structure of rules, with the most powerful people at the top. I say HIERARCHY, you say:*
> Whole class: *HIERARCHY!*
> Miss Adams: *I say HIERARCHY, you say…*
> Whole class: *HIERARCHY!*
> Miss Adams: *Maria, please can you state the word and then give us a definition.*
> Maria: *HIERARCHY – something about rules, Miss?*
> Miss Adams: *'Archy' means rule, yes, but Samon, what does the term 'hierarchy' mean?*
> Samon: *A clear structure of rules, Miss.*
> Miss Adams: *Maria, what does 'hierarchy' mean?*
> Maria: *A clear structure of rules, Miss.*

I want to unpick a few things about this routine.

Firstly, it is vital that this choral response is practised until it becomes second nature. Students may be shy at first, or shout out to mask their discomfort. Tackle this quickly.

Secondly, your team might find this a little contrived, but again, the 'why' is crucial. So many students – particularly those new to English – need to hear, practise and pronounce a word that they may only have read. I still remember discovering my inability to pronounce

Hermione from the *Harry Potter* series correctly after someone said the name aloud. I had spent years pronouncing this as *her – me – own*.

Finally, remember the power of culture. If this is happening in every lesson, every day, it will become habitual for our students and, most importantly, they will learn more and remember more, turning into articulate and vocabulary-rich young adults.

7. Cold-calling

Cold-calling is when the teacher chooses which student responds and it could be anyone.

For teachers, this can be contentious. Reasonable adjustments should be made for students, but this is likely to apply only to a minority of students within your school.

> **Routine:** Teachers should use cold-calling as their default mode of questioning students throughout a lesson.

I believe cold-calling can be an effective routine for building a culture of excellence. This is how it looks in practice.

There are two essential ingredients to ensure that this routine is effective in the classroom:

1. wait time
2. placing students' names at the end of the question.

Of course, cold-calling is only effective in the right classroom environment. A culture of error is fundamental in ensuring that this routine works well.

As teachers, we are so often concerned with students actively avoiding errors, mistakes or misunderstandings; however, this solution is actually focused on creating a 'culture of error', which enables a teacher to efficiently ensure that every learner in the classroom is truly understanding the lesson content.

A significant way in which to do this is to shift the mindset of the teacher – even breaking ingrained habits where necessary – to ensure that the right culture and learning environment permeates the room, focusing on checking understanding for everyone.

Sherrington (2019) suggests these useful examples of such a shift in mindset:

- from *Does anyone know?* to *Does everyone know?*
- from *Can anyone do it?* to *Can everyone do it?*
- from *Well done to those getting it right* to *Let's find out who still can't get this right and help them out.*

This shift in teachers' communication with learners is incredibly powerful, but it needs to be embedded deeply within the pedagogy of a teacher and become habitual. This does not work if applied on a superficial level or if only deployed infrequently.

This must be the mindset every single time:

How do I, as a teacher, ensure that every student in my class knows the answer to these questions? How do I avoid an illusory notion of assessing all students' understanding?

Consider again my bell task (Recall 6) from routine three earlier.

With tasks such as these, the instinct may be to pose questions in the vein of *Does anyone know the answer for question 1?* or perhaps cold-call and select a student, e.g. *Jake, what did you get for question 1?*, followed by congratulations to Jake for a correct answer and a cursory acknowledgement to the other learners of *Did you all get that?*, followed by a few nods. I may feel that my students understand because I have heard a correct answer – but the problem is that this is so often not the case. Even those students who fill in blank pages retrospectively after Jake's offering have not actually learned much, except how to avoid my attention as their teacher.

Then, after working our way through the questions, we might ask the students to tell us their score. *OK, Year 10, hands up if you got*

6/6… 4/6… 2/6, etc. However, this is such a poor proxy of gauging the understanding of learners – but it happens all the time! (If it has not happened to you, I do not believe you!)

We need to find the errors, the gaps, the mistakes first.

This is how I changed my mindset when giving feedback on this task, in order to instil a culture of error and ensure that everyone in the classroom knew the answers to these questions by the end of the feedback session.

After the allotted time elapsed, I asked students to put their pens down, close their books and face the board, and I framed the feedback session with:

> *Thank you, Year 10. Now, I am not interested in those of you who got the right answers. I am far more interested in those who perhaps have a gap in their responses today. I would imagine that perhaps questions 1 and 4 might have been a struggle for you. Hands up those of you who did not get an answer for those…*

Notice how I made it OK – almost expected for some students – not to have a correct answer in their books. This worked well and six hands were raised. I praised this with a simple 'good'. It is vital to see gaps in learning as part of the experience and view them with positivity, as students know that they will be addressed soon. I then continued with:

> *Of course, there may be other gaps too. So, let's find out who has not got the correct answers and help them out. Fraser, let's see whether you can help everyone to understand the answer to question 1. Please open your book and tell us your answer. Everyone else, open your books too, as Fraser is going to help us all. Pop your hand up if you had a gap for question 1… Fraser is going to help the six of you with gaps to make sure that everyone understands this answer. The rest of you should be ready to do the same with the next questions too, where you can.*

Of course, Fraser was a deliberate choice in the cold-call – I knew that he had the answer, but I wanted the atmosphere to be a supportive one, where students help everyone to know something. I had already made it clear that I wanted to seek out gaps in their learning, and the lesson's focus shifted to helping everyone out.

A similar process followed for the feedback for questions 2 to 5, and we all had the goal of making sure that everyone understood.

The process ended with me posing this question to a series of students: *Does everyone now know the answers to the questions? Jack? Abbie? Becky?* Perhaps due to the culture in the classroom, Becky actually responded (unprompted by me) by addressing the class: *Can you confirm that you have all the answers now? I don't think Mr Hale will move on until everyone does.*

This is not a perfect example of a lesson. This is not the finished article. But this shift in teacher mindset towards the deliberate intent of 'Can everyone do it?' is essential if we are going to begin to address this problem in teaching.

8. Do not allow students to paraphrase answers verbally

You may not have experienced this in the classroom, but it is a HUGE bugbear of mine.

Imagine that you ask the students to write down a response to the question 'How does Scrooge juxtapose Fezziwig?'.

Here's what the student writes (a real example):

> *Whilst Scrooge is presented as a miser who exploits his clerk, Fezziwig is presented as his antithesis: a benevolent and generous boss.*

Here's what the student says (a real example):

> *So, um, it's sorta like Scrooge is a miser who is a rubbish boss, whilst Fezziwig is far more benevolent.*

Students have an odd habit sometimes of thinking that we are asking them to paraphrase a written response or verbalise an answer from memory when called on. NO. NO. NO.

> **Routine:** Teachers should always model answering in full sentences and insist that students do this at all times.

If I am to develop academic register in oral as well as written responses, I must insist on the students reading out the answer EXACTLY AS IT IS WRITTEN ON THE PAGE. This has a huge benefit to the whole class, who are then steeped in the academic language that underpins strong writing.

Final thoughts

There will, of course, be more routines that I establish, but these are the examples that have had the greatest impact on my practice and will hopefully allow you to reflect upon your own.

To get you thinking even more deeply about the power of habits and routines, I want to end this chapter with two case studies.

The first is from James Dyke, a trust leader for English and instruction at Dixons Academies, and formerly head of English at Dixons Trinity Chapeltown (DTC), Leeds. He masterfully exemplifies the power of habits and routines from the perspective of a teacher. And let me tell you – it really works! In 2023, DTC students made exceptional progress in English literature and language, placing the school in the top six nationally for the progress of disadvantaged students.

The second case study is from Shabnam Ahmed, who writes wonderfully about the habitual learner. This offers an interesting extension of the ideas from James's case study, where she considers how students can also become masters of habits to enable success.

Case study: Building a culture of excellence through habits and routines

James Dyke

Often, as teachers and department leads, we possess *that* meticulously planned, intelligently sequenced curriculum. The PowerPoints and booklets are beautiful. The Tier 2 and Tier 3 vocabulary is explicitly mapped out. We have a strong team of good teachers. Perhaps classroom culture is perfectly fine. We have brushed up on our subject knowledge.

And yet students aren't doing as well as they could. Are they working hard enough? Are they confident and quick to start their essays? Is every student, particularly the most vulnerable, punching above their weight?

The phenomenal achievements of our students were not an accident – I firmly believe that much of the winning formula came from a couple of 'intangibles':

- their joy for the subject
- their motivation to master the subject.

A piece of feedback that visitors always give about English lessons is 'but the students seem to love English – they seem so engaged in learning'. This is not a happy accident. After many years of trying to get students to 'love' English, I figured that, ultimately, it came down to a simple concept: create the conditions in which students can learn and thrive in your subject, and then the joy will come. These conditions, if you will, come about through unglamorous hard work – a core value of our school. The nuts and bolts of these conditions – the small, everyday stuff – revolved around:

- consistency of teaching/instruction, in every classroom, every day (this does not mean rigid, inflexible, identical or robotic – it simply means that the expectations are high everywhere and are unsurprising to students)

- habits of excellence, fostered in our students through expert modelling of the subject domain
- tight routines that facilitate learning and give room to learning the stuff that matters most – we explain to students that we are dogmatic about the small things so that they can pay attention to the complex matter of English!

In order to truly push students from good to great, we need to build habits of excellence and use routines effectively. As is often written about in school culture or behaviour blogs, habits and routines are essential for creating the enabling conditions for learning. I have written about these two facets for the Bradford Research School:

- Behavioural routines create more time and space for learning.
- Instructional routines make learning more efficient.

At DTC, we leave nothing to chance. Below are some examples of what we put in place to foster excellence.

Enabling conditions

Whilst not explicitly habits or routines, the following conditions are in place at a school-wide or system level. These conditions are crucial for allowing teachers to teach and students to learn, and cannot go without mention.

- **A centralised behaviour system:** This means that students are held to the same expectations in every lesson.
- **A centrally planned, booklet-resourced curriculum:** I won't go into the benefits of booklets, but a centrally planned curriculum ensures a level of rigour and consistency across the department, and prevents the over-work of individual teachers in perpetually recreating resources. Equally, the curriculum needs to be tailored to the class – it is not rigid and inflexible.

- **Common, school-wide language:** Narration of positive affirmations, expectations and mantras allows students to feel a sense of belonging and that all teachers value them and hold them to the same expectations.

Habits and routines in English

At Dixons, we talk often of aligned autonomy – the optimal balance between consistency and self-determination. Alignment in your team is a powerful lever that we should not be afraid to pull:

- What does a typical English lesson look like for your team?
- What classroom routines does every teacher use in order to facilitate great learning?
- What (good!) habits will students pick up from your English teachers that will allow them to find more time for deeper, more complex learning?

As a leader, you must set your stall out on these conditions. Not only are we creating equitable outcomes for students, but we are also being fair in support of all our staff. Sometimes, it may feel uncomfortable to be 'aligned' or insistent on consistency, but if the right things are consistent, then it benefits everyone.

A caveat: what I am talking about is principles of great teaching and classroom practice in English. It is important to understand which principles are important and why, and focus on outcome over performative process.

The following routines and habits helped to 'supercharge' our students, starting with some familiar instructional routines and followed by more curriculum-based, subject-specific habits.

Starts to lessons

The 'do now' activity: We decided that its purpose in English was to facilitate the retrieval of the core knowledge that all students needed and to limit any forgetting. This principle was uniform across our team. Some other core principles that we stuck to included:

- retrieval of core declarative knowledge every lesson (co-constructed by the team)
- retrieval of vocabulary and academic phrasing
- quotation recall in literature
- a blend of recall and short application (where relevant/useful).

Mini-whiteboards (MWBs)

This is a universal method of checking for understanding that has been around for a while, and yet I see many English departments shy away from their use. We created specific routines (that were underpinned by the whole school) around how, when and why we would use mini-whiteboards in English:

- **Do now:** Every 'do now' activity is completed on an MWB – every staff member actively checks student responses, meaning that they can quickly glean what students know or don't.
- **Vocabulary drilling:** Every staff member uses MWBs when teaching students new words.
- **Sentence drafting:** English, as a long-form subject, doesn't always lend itself to the writing of full responses on MWBs; however, it is powerful to break down longer responses and explicitly teach sentence formation, paragraph structure or simply the organising of ideas in an academic sentence. MWBs allow this rehearsal, practice, redrafting and checking, before moving on.

Turn, talk, write, feedback

Whilst our approach to teaching English is very didactic and sees the teacher as an expert, it would be a misconception to assume that students are lectured to and silent for the whole time. In order to build good habits of thinking, discussion and debate, we regularly build in opportunities for the following, usually used in a 'stacked' manner:

- turn and talk – short, sharp, focused bursts of discussion
- everybody writes – an opportunity to jot down thoughts in a low-stakes manner
- feedback through no-hands-up questioning
- opportunities to raise a hand to build on, question or challenge a response.

Whilst not all of these strategies are by any means revolutionary, their tight and routine use (often modelled in department meetings by a teacher) means that students become accustomed to thinking hard about the content, feeling supported in discussing and working through challenging questions, and also know that they will be expected to contribute, upping accountability.

Common approach to modelling

We live-model every aspect of the curriculum, so that students can see an expert guide them through the knowing before the doing. We narrate everything that we do aloud, including mistakes, changes and sporadic mid-paragraph thoughts, so that students can pick up these same habits in their exams.

- **Guided practice through a loose form of 'I do, we do, you do':** We decide as a team how we should model certain responses, what we want students to do and when, and how this might be adapted for certain groups of students.
- **Student accountability:** This is a common approach to what students should do during a period of modelling. Every student is supported to watch and listen to the live model, is held to account for this attention and is then instructed to practise collectively or individually at the appropriate moment.

Terminology

In order to teach to the top, we ensure consistency around the language, concepts and vocabulary that we introduce to students and expect them to learn, including:

- which key terminology will be taught and when
- which concepts students will encounter and what they mean
- which phrasing should be used when analysing
- which vocabulary and phrasing should be used when writing about texts.

The explicit teaching and modelling of these elements of the curriculum is repetitive and consistent across the whole year group. Reference to phrasing and terms has become commonplace, with students ultimately using it in their writing organically.

Feedback

At DTC, we give feedback every lesson and we tell the students that it is a gift. We also tell them that hard work involves acting on next steps and refining our work – this is what the experts do! Below are the ways in which we give feedback in every lesson:

- **'Review now':** Following the 'do now' activity, the teacher selects one high-leverage common misconception/error on which to feed back.
- **Live feedback during independent practice:** Students are accustomed to teachers circulating, hunting for specific successes, next steps, misconceptions and errors (which have been rigorously pre-planned for) in their work.
- **'Show call':** Feedback and refinement are normalised through the strategic deployment of student work under a visualiser, so that, collectively, we can improve or celebrate the work. The same routine is used by the teacher and the same habits worked on by students:

- What successes does my work have that the teacher is identifying?
- Have I made any little mistakes or errors? How has the teacher corrected it?
- How will I refine an aspect of my work, as shown by the teacher, to push it from good to great?

Worried about students not reacting well to this? It's all in the phrasing/delivery. Normalise it in the culture, and the students will always rise to the challenge.

- **Whole class feedback:** This is a longer-form feedback and redrafting of selected pieces of work, such as whole essays.

Facilitating consistency and excellence – the department meeting

A challenge that every leader faces is to ensure a level of alignment in their team. We use department time as a way of creating the conditions for learning and curriculum implementation, based around the following principles:

- zero admin (this is reserved for emails/bulletins)
- deliberate practice of routines/pedagogical approaches modelled by leaders
- Co-construction of responses/co-planning/curriculum mapping.

Case study: Developing the habitual learner – the 'hows' and 'whys' of habitual learning

Shabnam Ahmed

Habits are a repeated behaviour that we subconsciously carry out during our day. We lean on habits, whether good or bad, and they form the routines of our day. Children are equally reliant on habits, and some of those habits are beneficial for learning, whilst others can hinder the learning that takes place. As teachers, it is our job (and skill) to decipher which habits are paramount to developing excellent learners.

To build healthy and effective habits, the everyday routines of the classroom must be worked on continuously, and revisited and reflected upon regularly. A learned behaviour that becomes automatic has a very delicate balance, where, if tipped – for example, a change in environment or falling back into older habits – it can shift the way in which students work. It is imperative that when building habits, they are frequently revisited and insisted upon; otherwise, there is a risk of disrupting the pathway towards creating automatic learners. There is, of course, a caveat, where habits can sometimes stunt creativity, but in the most part the foundational habits, i.e. the behaviours for learning, are beneficial to creating effective learning time.

To support my understanding and implementation of good study habits, I undertook some initial research on how habits are formed and what interventions we can apply to ensure that the best habits are implemented. I used a range of sources to help me with my understanding, such as:

- *Atomic Habits* by James Clear (2018): This is a really easy read, which can help anyone to understand the conception of habits, how to rewrite them and ways in which to maintain them. I would recommend this, due to the ease of read.
- *The Handbook of Behavior Change*, edited by Martin S. Hagger et al. (2020): This is a brilliant book, packed with lots of studies based on behaviour change and interventions. It's given me a lot of food for thought.

How I developed the habitual learner

When I first joined my school in 2022, I was given a Key-Stage-4-heavy timetable. I had to learn the systems of the school and the names of the children and work out where each of those students were on the learning line. The only way in which I felt that I could move forward in an effective way was to strip back and think of the habits that I wanted my students to develop.

These all started with behaviour for learning habits – how students behaved during learning time and how cemented these patterns were. In the first few weeks, I discovered that there were not any concrete habits in place and that students were struggling with cognitive load and enjoyment in the lesson. They didn't feel successful and therefore were not encouraged to push themselves, nor were they ready to undertake/continue their GCSE course.

I knew that this wasn't isolated to just my classes, based on an attempt to lead a 'walking talking mock'. Previously, the school had undertaken a rocky journey, with recovering from Covid, having several supply teachers working across the school, a change of leadership and moving into a trust and then (a successful) Ofsted. I didn't want to rock the boat further, having been appointed as the new head of faculty and already making changes to the curriculum. I decided that I'd experiment in my own classes.

I still found this an overwhelming task, and sought solace in James Clear's *Atomic Habits*, which taught me at a basic level what habits were and how they were formed. It gave me clarity in how I would attempt to develop habitual learners, but I had to use my own experience as a teacher to identify the missing habitual behaviours.

As I penned down the habits that I wanted students to have, I thought only about what the impact would be. It all started with marginal gains – how could I make my students one per cent better every day, so that they could gradually develop into the best versions of themselves?

I started with the following things:

1. 'do now' tasks
2. cold-calling
3. questioning and responses.

Through reading *The Handbook of Behavior Change*, I learned all about how human behaviour is created. In chapter two: Changing

Behavior Using the Theory of Planned Behaviour, three elements are outlined as guiding behaviour:

- beliefs about one's ability to carry out the behaviour
- beliefs about what important others think should be done
- beliefs about the likely consequences of behaviour.

This made me realise that control is the key to strengthening and carrying out intentions. If you know why and how behaviour patterns are created, you can then begin to intervene with the process to ensure that the best habits are developed. It meant that I had to really know my classes and could only perform interventions if I knew what the barrier was for many students. In the first instance, however, I needed to work out what was going to take place in my classroom and when.

As a result, I moved onto marking out exactly when I wanted each habit to take place. I thought about cues that I could put into place to ensure that students would behave automatically. This all began at the classroom door, where I would greet and direct students to the first thing that I wanted them to do – the 'do now' task. This required relentless observation and reminders to complete the work. I coupled this with using cold-calling, so that all students knew that at some point I'd be looking for their answers. It seems very basic, but when I shared with my students what I was doing, I made it clear that the 'craving' for them would be to be able to contribute in the cold-calling or class discussion. I even introduced extrinsic rewards, such as stickers, because I knew that it would serve as a motivator for students.

After a while, I could see the quick wins that I had made here, with one student identifying it as the best part of his day because he felt instant success. This is when I knew that I could apply this methodology to just about anything. The key to it all, though, was to identify the habit (with the end goal), break down the process and then be transparent with my students. For every habit that I wanted them to form, I told them the exact pathway for how they would get there.

Soon enough, I had students in my classes knowing about 60 quotations off by heart, ready for their exam. I made the habit easy to implement – it was only a quotation recall, with a word missing – and students could feel success almost instantaneously. This, as a result, gave them the perfect dopamine hit that they needed in order to make the habit much more alluring and, eventually, embedded.

I had students in my class automatically performing the behaviour for learning habits with very few prompts. It meant that we could solely focus on the content of English literature, and the lesson moved on much quicker.

My next step was to take this out of my own classroom and begin rolling it out department-wide. This involved looking at the schemes of learning and, together as a team, stripping back the resources, slides, etc. so that we could really focus on reducing cognitive load and developing effective behaviour for learning habits. We've now embedded all lessons with those simple habits, and our classrooms are calm, focused and purposeful. Every student knows what to expect when they come to English, and our results have improved significantly!

It's important not to be complacent, though, and as a team we are constantly revising how we ensure that the learning process is clear for our students and that those habits are simple but consistent.

Chapter 3
Upholding the law

This chapter covers:

- the need for quality assurance in your department
- effective systems to quality assure – or uphold the law – including deliberate practice, spotlights, book looks and the four Rs
- strategies for implementing each system successfully.

This chapter was originally titled 'Quality assurance'. However, as I discussed in Chapter 1 concerning the role of the leader and autonomy, the leader of the English department needs to ultimately establish the laws to which a department is to adhere. You need to hold yourself and those you lead accountable to these laws. This title felt like a more appropriate metaphor for what this chapter really entails.

In my experience, quality assurance – at least in education – seems to have become a dirty phrase. If it is, I would argue that this is perhaps more reflective of a toxic school or department culture. I have no problem with the phrase per se, but it does not capture what I set out earlier in the book as the vehicle in which to build a culture of excellence.

Upholding the law (which, remember, as a leader, you have written!) feels more palatable for such an aim. It reminds me of an acronym that underpins the culture that The Totteridge Academy in North London has created regarding staff development: WDWWSWD (We Do What We Say We Do).

In other words, as the leader of an English department, there are three key pillars to your role:

1. Establish what we do.
2. Enact what we do.
3. Ensure that we do what we say.

The combination of these three things ensures that you are upholding the law of your department.

What follows, is choosing suitable methods to ensure that this happens. Based on my experience across multiple English departments and schools, a combination of the following bears the greatest fruits:

- deliberate practice
- spotlights
- book looks
- the four Rs.

This chapter offers examples of how to implement each in turn. I have codified them and used language that is familiar to me. You may call them something else, but each should be a tool in your arsenal that you can use and make your own as you establish the law of your department.

Deliberate practice

A common problem with professional development sessions in schools is the 'knowing–doing gap' (Pfeffer and Sutton, 1999). Deliberate practice has proven to be an extremely effective form of professional development, which allows teachers to rehearse elements of their practice outside of the classroom before embedding them.

The term 'deliberate practice' itself was coined by Ericsson to describe a type of practice that 'is a highly structured activity, the explicit goal of which is to improve performance. Specific tasks are invented to overcome weaknesses, and performance is carefully monitored to provide cues for ways to improve it further' (Ericsson et al., 1993, p. 368). In Ericsson's *Peak: Secrets from the New Science of Expertise*, he further argues that 'The right sort of practice carried out over a sufficient period of time leads to improvement. Nothing else.' (Ericsson and Poole, 2016, p. 11). This is an important thing to communicate with your team. When you are upholding the law, your ultimate goal is to improve the practice of your team.

In other words, you will role-play delivering a specific lesson routine to your peers, who then offer constructive feedback to improve your practice. Deliberate practice allows you and your team to recreate classroom situations, so that teachers can learn to identify good decisions and to act upon them. From experience, I will say that it does take a little getting used to. It can feel embarrassing, and often staff have commented that, initially at least, they feel nervous doing this with their peers. However, it soon abates and is a really practical way in which to establish your mental model of a habit or routine that you want to uphold in your department.

At Trinity Academy Leeds, we benefit massively from a whole-school approach to deliberate practice. Our senior leadership team have really invested in this as a method of CPD, and it is woven into the fabric of the school, as evidenced below in this excerpt from our Expert Teaching at TAL policy document:

All teaching staff (including ITTs and ECTs) are assigned to a deliberate practice group, run by one of our six lead coaches. These sessions run once fortnightly, within the allocated CPD hour on staff timetables, and cover whole-school priorities identified by the Teaching and Learning team through spotlights and drop-ins.

Even if your school does not have a system like this, as the leader of your English department you can absolutely use this both to set the standards of your habits and routines and also in a remedial way to develop your team's practice.

In Chapter 8, I tend to include deliberate practice in every department meeting as a culture *critique*. From my lesson drop-ins and spotlights of the department, I identify areas where deliberate practice of a particular routine might be required to ensure that it is delivered expertly by all members of the team.

For now, let me illustrate an example of how deliberate practice will enable you to uphold the law of your department.

Imagine that you realise that several members of your team are allowing students to paraphrase their written answers verbally after being cold-called. Deliberate practice can act as a timely reminder before a habit becomes too ingrained into a teacher's practice and can offer the opportunity to rehearse this routine prior to employing it in their classroom.

How you frame this is important if your department are going to recognise the importance of upholding the law. Here is how I would introduce deliberate practice for this particular situation:

> *Thank you for allowing me into your classrooms this week. There were some exceptional examples of our habits and routines being implemented. For example, all of us are creating that healthy tension in wait time during cold-calling to ensure both high participation and thinking ratio during questioning. However, one thing I noticed was that on several occasions students were breaking the law… they were allowed to paraphrase written answers when responding verbally. We are going to use deliberate practice to make sure that we all feel confident about how to ensure that students always respond in an academic register.*

I begin with gratitude for entering the department's classroom. This is a privilege that you have a leader, and you need to mirror that in your language. I then make it clear that there were examples of excellence in *another* routine, so that the department recognises where they have upheld the law and it is appreciated. The final section is about building a culture where teachers understand that there will always be improvements that could be made in their practice, but that I am offering practicable support to achieve both ours and their goals.

The deliberate practice session should then be structured as follows:

1. The department leader steps into role (where the team acts as students) and delivers an example of how the routine should be used in the classroom.
   I am going to imagine that I will ask a Year 7 student – Sam, please can you be the student – to read their answer to the question 'How does Scrooge juxtapose Fezziwig?'.
   Sam, please give an answer that clearly sounds like a paraphrase of a student's written answer. I will then show you all what you should do to correct the student so that they do not paraphrase; rather, they read their written answer aloud with confidence.
   Now, I am going to step into role…

   Teacher: *Right, Year 7, be ready to tell the class your answer to the question 'How does Scrooge juxtapose Fezziwig?'. How does Scrooge juxtapose Fezziwig… Sam?*

   Sam: *So, um, it's sorta like Scrooge is a miser who is a rubbish boss, whilst Fezziwig is far more benevolent.*

   Teacher: *Let's try again, Sam. To be clear, I do not want you to try to answer from memory. I want you to read EXACTLY what you wrote in your booklet. Thank you.*

   Sam: *Whilst Scrooge is presented as a miser who exploits his clerk, Fezziwig is presented as his antithesis: a benevolent and generous boss.*

   Teacher: *Much better, Sam. It was great to hear brilliant academic language like 'antithesis'.*

2. The department leader then seeks feedback from the department, both on what went well and also on how this could be improved upon.

   Deliberate practice leader: *What went well, do you think? Any tweaks to improve?*

   Staff member 1: *I liked the fact that you were really clear in the expectation – especially in the way that you emphasised they should read out what they wrote EXACTLY.*

> Staff member 2: *Yes, though I think you could have been a little warmer then. Maybe show why it's important to not paraphrase.*
>
> Staff member 3: *I really like it when we talk about the beautiful work our students do.*
>
> Deliberate practice leader: *That's helpful. I'll try to do that next time.*
>
> **3.** The department leader enacts the routine again in role, taking account of the feedback.
>
> Teacher: *Let's try again, Sam. To be clear, I do not want you to try to answer from memory. I want you to read EXACTLY what you wrote in the beautiful answer that you wrote in your booklet. Thank you.*
>
> **4.** Further feedback and discussion should take place to critique the routine and address any queries or concerns and tackle any misconceptions.
>
> Staff member 2: *Just to be really clear, even if the student is nervous or struggles to read aloud, do we ask them to keep trying to do this?*
>
> Deliberate practice leader: *Absolutely. All students are able to do this – we need to lift them up so that they can. As you said earlier, it is about being warm in the way in which we do this.*
>
> **5.** Another member of the department steps into role and practises the routine, and the steps above are repeated. Continue to do this with all members of the department, where necessary.

As the leader, you need to embody the mental model, but also accept and be responsive to the feedback given. This is why you must go first. You need to set the culture of how deliberate practice is used in your department through actions and not words.

Consider why this is such a benefit in supporting your team to uphold the laws of a department:

- There is time and space to reflect upon one's practice in a low-stakes environment.
- Feedback is immediate and acted upon straight away.
- The whole department witnesses how you uphold the law, and the mental model that you hold becomes stronger across a range of staff members.
- You can lead by example and act as a role model for your team.

Spotlights

In this section, I want to make a distinction between lesson spotlights and more informal lesson observation methods, often referred to as learning walks or drop-ins.

I always insist on an open-door policy when it comes to staff members or visitors watching me teach – or indeed, the members of my department. Regular, low-stakes observation is far more useful and less stressful than infrequent formal lesson observations.

How often you informally observe members of your department will depend on your capacity. Personally, I aim to pop into lessons each day where possible, and certainly on a weekly basis (even if this is very briefly). This approach allows you to inform deliberate practice sessions.

Thankfully, as a profession, we have ditched individual grades for lesson observations. The idea that someone can be issued a grade based on a single observation of their teaching is ludicrous, but it is something that was very normalised when I first trained as a teacher.

As a newly qualified teacher I was observed by a teacher who graded my lesson as a 3 (satisfactory) because the students were *too quiet* and the lesson lacked a *buzz*. I was gutted. I was encouraged to observe the teacher who had observed me, to witness how to be better…

There was a buzz, certainly – lots of discussion, in comparison to my rather silent lesson beyond questioning. The problem was that this was mainly off-task talk. I still remember how a pair of students, who were meant to be working collaboratively on a series of simultaneous equations, had a whole conversation about what they were going to order from *Nando's* that Friday evening.

I do not recount this anecdote to disparage that teacher, but rather to make it clear that you should never observe an English lesson delivered by a member of your department and attempt to award a grade. This is because a snapshot of a lesson observed can never form a holistic judgement of a teacher's performance.

However, in my experience, lesson observations often miss a key ingredient that really allows you as a leader to know how well your curriculum is being enacted by your department.

Often, lesson observations consist of a teacher watching another teacher at the back of the room. They might walk around a little or look in books, but it feels artificial. Observing should really be focused on the students and not the teacher.

Lesson spotlights with an in-built system for student voice can be a much better way in which to check how well the English curriculum is being delivered. After all, the students are the ones learning the curriculum.

There are a variety of ways to do this, but below is an example of how you might systematise lesson spotlights:

Lesson spotlights with student feedback

Staff have at least one lesson spotlight every term. These are completed by the curriculum leader. During each spotlight, 'walk and talk' student feedback will take place, where a student is taken out of the lesson and asked a range of key questions about their learning from the list below:

1. What did you learn in the lesson that I visited today?
2. How did it link with what you have been studying recently?

> **3.** How do teachers teach you what you need to know?
> **4.** Thinking back to last year, I can see that you learned A, B, C and D. Choose one of these topics and tell me what you can remember. Have you used any of this learning this term?
> **5.** Tell me how your teachers plan learning that builds on what you already know.
> **6.** Show me a piece of work that you are proud of.
>
> In addition to lesson spotlights, curriculum leaders also conduct regular drop-ins to inform the holistic view of the quality of teaching and learning in their department.

The use of student voice here can be a very powerful tool. Notice how the questions reveal interesting answers about the impact of the curriculum delivery on the students. There is nothing vague or abstract about the questions – they are aligned with what you need to know about your curriculum:

- Are students building on their knowledge each lesson?
- Do they understand how the sequence of lessons supports the building of their knowledge over time?
- Can they articulate how teachers support them in their learning?
- What work have they produced that evidences their learning over time?

Book looks

Students' books (booklets, folders, whatever you use for students' written work) can be a powerful thing to use to check that your curriculum is having an impact. Again, as with student spotlights, this is because the students are the ones learning the curriculum.

TABLE 1: Book scrutiny indicators

Building on previous learning	Depth and breadth of coverage	Pupil progress	Practice
Pupils' knowledge is consistently, coherently and logically sequenced so that it can develop incrementally over time. There is a progression from the simpler and/or more concrete concepts to the more complex and/or abstract ones. Pupils' work shows that they have developed their knowledge and skills over time.	The content of the tasks and pupils' work show that pupils learn a suitably broad range of topics within a subject. Tasks also allow pupils to deepen their knowledge of the subject by requiring thought on their part, understanding of subject-specific concepts and making connections to prior knowledge.	Pupils make strong progress from their starting points. They acquire knowledge and understanding appropriate to their starting points.	Pupils are regularly given opportunities to revisit and practise what they know to deepen and solidify their understanding in a discipline. They can recall information effectively, which shows that learning is durable. Any misconceptions are addressed and there is evidence to show that pupils have overcome these in future work.

(Taken from Ofsted, 2019, p. 5)

The four key areas in Table 1 are a useful starting point to determine the impact that your curriculum has on students' written work. However, as the leader of an English department, your responsibility becomes taking this generic model of effective learning and ensuring that you can apply this to your subject specifically.

This method is not using book looks as a way in which to check teachers' marking, however. If your feedback and marking policy is clear, all you need to know about teachers' marking is whether or not they are following the policy.

This method is about how you can use students' books as evidence of an effective enaction of your curriculum and what you as a leader can learn about how your department is delivering that curriculum.

Below are some specific examples within an English curriculum that might be useful to investigate further as part of a book look:

1. Building on previous learning

The work that you see in students' books shows a journey of students' learning. Look at how previous work informs more recent work and how that supports future learning.

For example, imagine that Year 7 are studying Gothic writing during a term. The end-point of the unit is students' own writing in the Gothic genre, inspired by the works of Gothic literature that they have been studying.

Your curriculum should be well sequenced to best prepare students for the end-point review; therefore, students' books should clearly evidence that. The evidence that you are tracking in your book look might follow a pattern like this:

> At the beginning of the unit, students have secured knowledge of what a noun, verb, adjective and adverb are, as the prerequisite knowledge required to use modification in their writing. As we move through the students' work, we can see

> the application of this knowledge in their writing – students begin to use simple ADJECTIVE + NOUN structures, but as they grow and develop this becomes more complex. Students develop their writing through the use of adjectival phrases and even begin to use expansion to add complexity to sentence forms during descriptions of specific nouns within their dark, atmospheric settings.

2. Depth and breadth of curriculum coverage

Again, this is driven by your curriculum design, but the 'book look' is useful to see how the depth and breadth of your curriculum is enacted by students in their work.

For example, if you are teaching Shakespeare's *Romeo and Juliet*, what does depth and breadth of coverage look like? Students' work, of course, needs to strike a balance between the two. You might have a specific focus on Romeo's attitudes to love, say, but I would be looking for the following to determine adequate depth and breadth of coverage in that case:

- Are students able to use a wide range of textual evidence to illustrate Romeo's differing attitudes to love? Or are they only familiar with a couple of key scenes?
- Do they fully understand the change in Romeo's attitudes in Act 1? For example, his repeated references to how 'fair' Rosaline is in 1.1 and the contradiction upon seeing Juliet in 1.5?
- When exploring Shakespeare's language, do students rely too heavily on de-contextualised word-level analysis of key scenes ('Juliet is the sun') or are they recognising patterns of Shakespeare's language (e.g. light imagery – not just 'sun' but also 'torches', 'stars', 'bright angel', etc.)?

This might seem very specific, but that is the point. Remember that the books are just the evidence of the curriculum in action; they act as a mirror reflecting the curriculum back to you as the curriculum leader.

3. Pupils' progress

I always find this aspect most challenging. There is a subjectivity to evaluating progress that is often influenced by internalised expectations of you as leader, of the students' teacher and of the students themselves. What does 'strong progress' look like for an individual student, versus a particular cohort of students in English?

Regardless of students' starting points, I would expect to see in students' books a degree of mastery of the core knowledge set out through my curriculum from all students.

For example, if my book look was focused on literary analysis, I might have the following progress markers in mind for students with differing levels of prior attainment.

Low prior attainers:

- clear evidence of using a thesis statement to set up the main idea of a paragraph
- attempts to ensure that the POINT and QUOTATION from the thesis statement complement each other
- clear evidence of language exploration – students explaining how an author's choice of language helps to create meaning
- attempts to consider the wider authorial intent (the 'why').

Mid prior attainers:

- clear evidence of using a thesis statement to set up the main idea of a paragraph
- the POINT and QUOTATION from the thesis statement clearly complementing each other
- clear evidence of language exploration – students explaining how an author's choice of language helps to create meaning
- clear evidence of students examining the wider authorial intent (the 'why').

High prior attainers:

- the thesis statement being used to develop a LINE OF ARGUMENT
- a wider range of textual evidence (perhaps through QUOTATION) used throughout and not limited to that from the thesis statement
- clear evidence of language exploration – students explaining how an author's choice of language helps to create meaning
- clear evidence of students examining the wider authorial intent (the 'why').

These statements are very specific to a particular curriculum model. What you look for from students at different starting points will depend on what you have taught explicitly through *your* curriculum. As a leader, though, you must have this mental model at the forefront of your mind if you are going to speak with colleagues with confidence about whether or not you feel that students are making strong progress with your colleagues.

4. Practice

It's important to remember that learning is cumulative. Just because a student has written a beautiful piece of writing by the end of the lesson, this does not mean that they have learned how to do that forever and ever. A reminder: learning occurs when there is a change to the long-term memory.

This is where a book look becomes incredibly useful to evaluate how well students learn from your curriculum *over time*.

To best exemplify what you might look for as a leader in this area of the book look, I will break down each statement and offer an example of each in action for a potential English curriculum.

> *Pupils are regularly given opportunities to revisit and practice what they know to deepen and solidify their understanding in a discipline.*

If students are studying *Animal Farm* and your curriculum model means that you want students to understand how the novel acts as an allegory for the Russian Revolution, do your books mirror that?

If you witness students writing about how the animals' overthrow of Jones in Chapter 2 allegorises the proletariats' overthrow of Czar Nicholas II in 1917, but there are no further references to allegory when students are examining Napoleon's show trials in Chapter 7, have they deepened their understanding? This might be a fair question to ask about your curriculum. Do you need to perhaps add more contextual details about Stalin's period of 'Great Terror' in order to solidify students' understanding?

They can recall information effectively, which shows that learning is durable.

Many English lessons will have elements of recall, perhaps as a starter activity/'do now'. If so, this is something that is worth tracking during a book look.

For instance, a student who struggled to recall the definition of 'patriarchy' at the beginning of a unit of work is later not only able to recall what it is, but you can also see them using the word confidently in their interpretations of a text. This might provide evidence that their learning of this concept has become durable over time.

Any misconceptions are addressed and there is evidence to show that pupils have overcome these in future work.

Seek out mistakes that students make and then consider whether these mistakes are rectified over time. This is a powerful tool with which to evidence effective teaching and learning within your department.

For example, perhaps you notice that students had been continually failing to use the possessive apostrophe correctly in their work (e.g. Macbeth's ambition, Priestley's socialist ideology, etc.) until a point in their books where clearly the teacher identified this. Perhaps the teacher did a feedback session and students corrected their work and rectified their errors. This is great, but it is now worth checking whether the mistakes were made again following teacher feedback. If not, it is useful to consider how well your curriculum helps to support students in avoiding this literacy error.

Tread carefully with book look scrutiny

Of course, looking at students' work will have limitations. With any tool that you are using to uphold the law, intent is key and the intent should always be to check whether all members of your team are doing what you have agreed to do as a department. Any other preferences, notions or ideas that you have outside of this need to be firmly left outside the door.

Whenever you mention book looks to an English teacher, the issue of what effective marking looks like in English arises.

There are a multitude of approaches to marking in English but, fundamentally, my view always remains the same. In a recruitment and retention crisis, we cannot make marking in English a burdensome task to the point where teachers leave the profession. As a leader, you are responsible for making the marking workload manageable for your team.

One thing that is crystal clear to me: if you are asking members of your department to take piles of books home to mark in the evenings and weekends, due to a demand to write individual written comments in *every* book, you are not supporting your team's workload.

In 2016, the Education Endowment Foundation (EEF) published 'A marked improvement? A review of the evidence on written marking'. In a stark moment in the report, the reader is explicitly told: 'The quality of existing evidence focused specifically on written marking is low.' (Elliott et al., 2016, p. 5) Yet it is still a pervasive force in many English departments in the UK.

So, what are the alternatives? My experiences have led me to firmly believe that whole-class feedback and variations of this should be the proposed marking strategy in any English department. Establish a clear model for what your English department's marking system will look like, and the book look, provides a means to check that this model has been upheld.

The whole-class feedback approach is explored in Chapter 10 as a method to relieve the marking burden for members of your department.

Assessment reflection: the four Rs

Whenever your department has completed summative assessment, use this as a moment to reflect on how well your curriculum is being implemented and the impact that it is having on students' progress and outcomes.

The timing of this reflection tool will very much depend on your school's context (it might be following an exam week, mock examination window or end-of-unit test), but the principles will apply whenever you feel that it is apt to use it as a leader.

The tool can be summarised as the four Rs.

Reward	Recall
Reteach	Replan

FIGURE 2: The four R's

- **Reward:** Identify key knowledge strengths. What specific core concepts/knowledge from your curriculum have the vast majority of students mastered?
- **Recall:** Identify knowledge that needs quick recall. Students mostly understood the core concept, but this needs to be revisited briefly.
- **Reteach:** Identify key knowledge that needs reteaching. What specific core concepts/knowledge from your curriculum have the vast majority of students failed to master?

- **Replan:** Identify key knowledge that needs replanning in order to move forward, i.e. your major concerns or misconceptions that may have come about due to teaching or the curriculum design.

Using the four Rs captures what went well post-assessment and key areas of development moving forward, and helps signpost plans that you intend to action in order to address concerns.

Below is an example of how I have used this following a Key Stage 3 exam week. The language is very school- and curriculum-specific, but it should give you a sense of how it works in practice.

Reward

- I am impressed with Year 8 students' knowledge of poetic devices – they are even able to put these into action through their own compositions.
- Most students have demonstrated mastery of thesis statements to allow them to make valid POINTs (interpretations) of literary texts. This will strengthen students for AO1 when they begin the GCSE course.

Recall

- We need to include more examples of metaphor in Recall 6, drawing out students' knowledge of vehicle in particular and a vehicle's intended effect.
- Questions regarding LANGUAGE EXPLORATION need to be drip-fed into Recall 6 to remind students to explore authorial language choices where apt to do so in literary analysis.

Reteach

- Year 7s still need more explicit teaching of thesis statements – how/when to use them and why. This will be addressed in our spiral curriculum in their study of *Romeo and Juliet* in Term 6.
- Year 8s need to strengthen their LANGUAGE EXPLORATION.

- Year 9s need to be explicitly taught that the POINT is a LINE OF ARGUMENT and shown how the idea develops throughout a whole paragraph of literary analysis.

Replan

- We need to consider our subject-specific pedagogy when teaching creative writing to ensure that students write consciously for deliberate effect (especially High Prior Attaining (HPA) pupils) and don't just fulfil a sentence structure checklist.
- For the *Julius Caesar* booklet in 2024/25, we need to strip this down to focus more on exemplification of metaphor to depict Caesar's potential tyranny, to reinforce Golden Thread 5 (language, imagery and symbolism).

Part two

Curriculum, pedagogy and assessment

Chapter 4
Spiral curriculum and schema-building

This chapter covers:

- what a spiral curriculum is
- how to implement a spiral curriculum, through core concepts, disciplinary knowledge and explicit vocabulary instruction
- why a spiral curriculum builds students' schemas within English.

As an English lead, ensuring that you have the right curriculum in place for your school, your department and, most importantly, your students should be your highest priority. That's not to say that doing that alone will lead to excellence, but without it you are not able to excel in your department either.

How one views curriculum design can vary. Although I offer principles and examples of what I believe to be highly effective curriculum design, other methods could be just as successful. The enaction of a leader's clear, deep thinking is fundamental.

Early in my career, I did not always think too much – or very carefully – about curriculum design. In fact, conversations did not really go beyond text choices within an English curriculum. Of course, this will be part of the process, but often this becomes pre-eminent in all discussions around curriculum, and therefore becomes a mentality of staff adopting an English curriculum that is reductive.

Imagine that you or a member of your team were asked to discuss the sequencing of your curriculum – the 'what', the 'when' and the 'why' of particular choices. What would the response sound like? At the beginning of my career, it would have sounded very much like Scenario A below, but it has moved to Scenario B in recent years.

I have deliberately chosen a text that I taught at the very beginning of my career and which I added to my Key Stage 3 curriculum last year. In these scenarios, the imagined questioner asks the member of staff about why students are taught the novel *Purple Hibiscus* by Chimamanda Ngozi Adichie in Term 2 of Year 9. Below are each of the responses to this question.

Scenario A

The novel is highly engaging, but it contains mature themes such as domestic violence and the protagonist's sexual awakening, so it is more suited to Year 9 students. It is also more challenging as a text choice, so it is more likely to better prepare students for the demands of the GCSE exam.

Scenario B

The novel is an excellent vehicle with which to build upon students' prior learning in Key Stage 3. When we teach *Purple Hibiscus*, we examine the concepts of patriarchy and agency that stem from Eugene's fundamentalism. Earlier in our curriculum, students explore patriarchy and agency in their study of *Romeo and Juliet* and *I am Malala*. By revisiting these concepts through a different text, we are deepening students' knowledge of how these concepts present themselves through an increasingly challenging text choice.

You might read Scenario A and think that there is a clear justification of the text choice at this stage of the curriculum. You are right. However, it is superficial. It implies that the text was chosen based on engagement and age of students, rather than acting as a jigsaw piece in the overall puzzle that is a Key Stage 3 curriculum.

The thinking process in curriculum design

When leading secondary English, you have so much freedom and flexibility in what you teach and when you teach it at Key Stage 3. But, with great power comes great responsibility. A curricular choice at a particular moment should enmesh with the whole curriculum model. If it does not, it lacks coherence, which is vitally important when you consider the students' journey.

When first designing a curriculum, I always imagine this student journey. What will they learn in Key Stage 3 to set them up for success in Key Stage 4, Key Stage 5 and beyond? A useful way to do this is to track *backwards* in your curriculum design. This is more likely to elicit comments like those of Scenario B above.

So, what does that look like? Here's how I think about curriculum design, working from Key Stage 5 back to Key Stage 3.

Let's imagine that the following texts appear in your curriculum across each key stage. Again, these are texts that I have taught throughout my career, but they are also popular choices.

TABLE 2: Texts studied at each Key Stage

Key Stage 3	*I am Malala*, *Romeo and Juliet*, *Purple Hibiscus*
Key Stage 4	*An Inspector Calls*, *Macbeth*
Key Stage 5	*The Kite Runner*, *The Handmaid's Tale*

In a concept-led approach to curriculum planning, you must decide what high-leverage concepts should be explicitly taught in order to ensure that students have a deep understanding of the text and, in particular, authorial intent.

For all of the above, explicitly teaching the following two concepts is incredibly useful:

1. **Patriarchy:** a system of society in which men hold the power and women are largely excluded from it.
2. **Agency:** the ability to take action or choose what action to take.

A student learns these concepts through texts that allow them to deepen their understanding of the concepts and, in turn, the texts themselves.

In Key Stage 3, students are first introduced through their study of *I am Malala*, where they learn that under Taliban rule in Yousafzai's Swat Valley, women are not allowed to be educated or enter the public domain without a male chaperone, and they are forced to be covered almost entirely from head to toe. Due to the **patriarchal beliefs** of an extremist group, **all sense of agency for women is removed**. This concept is further reinforced when students study *Romeo* and *Juliet* and learn about **Juliet's lack of agency** over who she will marry, due to the **power and control held by the patriarch** of the Capulet household. Finally, the **cruel and abusive patriarch** of *Purple Hibiscus* also **removes Kambili's agency**. She is heavily restricted in her agency to forge a relationship with her so-called 'heathen' grandfather.

In Key Stage 4, students witness how **the patriarchal society of pre-war Britain** depicted in *An Inspector Calls* leads to **Birling's ability to exploit his female factory workers** and **limit their agency**, threatening redundancy if they do not accept his paltry pay offer. In *Macbeth*, the Witches plant the seed of ambition with the eponymous general in order to gain ultimate power. **He utilises his agency to commit regicide**, much to his bitter regret. And then there's the fiend-like Lady Macbeth – in a **deeply patriarchal world**, how are we to perceive her actions and the **motives that underly Duncan's murder?**

In Key Stage 5, students see the **toxic patriarchy** of the Taliban once more in *The Kite Runner,* and **the agency that is stripped from Sohrab**, forced into child prostitution. And, of course, is there a more brutal example than Gilead from *The Handmaid's Tale*, demonstrating the **erosion of female agency** in a world where **the patriarchy holds power over reproductive rights?**

In this thinking model above, the concepts of patriarchy and agency are intricately woven into the curriculum at each key stage to develop coherence, as well building a schema for students.

A 'spiral' curriculum

Many in the profession have (rightly) welcomed the recent shift to a forensic evaluation of a school or faculty's curriculum intent, implementation and impact by Ofsted in recent years. This has undoubtedly put a greater spotlight on curriculum design in schools, and the inspectorate offers a clear explanation as to its rationale for doing so:

> 'This inspection focus on curriculum is based on the insight from research into human cognition: if pupils don't succeed in learning what we hoped then they have knowledge gaps that will be preventing that success. When pupils are successful, the knowledge they need has built over time, allowing them to understand more complex ideas and undertake more complex tasks.' (Ofsted, 2021)

The English department at Trinity Academy Leeds is unashamedly academic and knowledge-rich in its design. It has also been sequenced to ensure that the 'knowledge [students] need has built over time, allowing them to understand more complex ideas and undertake more complex tasks' (Ofsted, 2021).

To achieve this lofty aim, we have adopted a 'spiral' approach to our curriculum in order to allow students to accrue powerful knowledge and, most importantly, to embed this in their long-term memory. After all, as Willingham succinctly asserts, 'memory is the residue of thought' (2010, p. 41). The way in which we accumulate knowledge, build schemas, learn things that we can do or use later and develop understanding is through thinking. As Sherrington notes in a blog, 'Thinking is the action; 'storage' of knowledge in memory is an outcome.' (Sherrington, 2021)

What is a 'spiral curriculum'?

The spiral curriculum is a cognitive theory proposed by Jerome Bruner (1960), which repeatedly revisits topics at increasing levels of difficulty. New skills and notions are 'clearly related to previous learning', with the aim of 'progressively increasing competency' (Harden, 1999, p. 141).

Revisiting key ideas repeatedly, spaced over time and interleaved with other learning, helps to embed them in long-term memory. This highlights the need to plan for such spacing to occur across several teaching units, phases or key stages.

'Spiral' approaches to curriculum design allows leaders to develop a curriculum model that is well sequenced to ensure that students know more and remember more. Myatt (2018) notes the importance of a curriculum being 'coherent'. Planning the curriculum across all levels can enable learning to be built upon effectively and links to be drawn throughout different phases and subject areas. Clare Sealy highlights that these links need to be 'meaningful, not forced' (Sealy, 2017). For example, if understanding the concept of female agency is essential to your curriculum, you might explicitly teach agency in a range of different texts with vastly different contexts.

A spiral curriculum leads to schema-building

A spiral curriculum is a cognitive theory. There is much debate in education regarding the role of cognitive science and how its principles can be harnessed into effective pedagogy. This is often quite contentious and polarising – particularly when it comes to applying cognitive science to the discipline of English.

Perhaps it is the reference to *science* that puts off English teachers from fully embracing this in their practice, or it might be something else. However, I can confirm that aspects of cognitive science have been revolutionary in my teaching practice in recent years.

One aspect that has been revelatory in shaping my approach to curriculum design is *schema-building*.

What is schema-building?

A *schema* describes a pattern of thought that organises categories of information and the relationships amongst them. In order for a student to retain and understand new information, they need to connect it to information that they already know. This is called *building a schema*.

Tom Sherrington (2020) expressed the importance of building a schema as being foundational to a teacher's practice:

'every student is piecing together ideas, information, experiences and concepts to form a coherent web that constitutes their understanding and fluency with the material in hand.'

Examples of schema-building in action

A well-designed curriculum should be driven by schema-building, and it is *every* teacher's responsibility to ensure that students are piecing together ideas and concepts to form a coherent web of the core knowledge that underpins their subject.

Below are several approaches to schema-building in an English curriculum.

1. Core concepts

One method of designing an English curriculum is through sequencing a range of core concepts (e.g. patriarchy or agency) that appear in a range of literary texts. For example, concepts may be built around universal themes from literature, such as:

TABLE 3: Common themes in literature

Heroism	Honour	Masculinity	Femininity
Hierarchy	Ambition	Morality	Inequality

This is *not* a definitive list and you may have a list with different concepts. Your thinking as a leader is key to developing the coherence in a curriculum model that allows the students' learning journey to build upon prior knowledge and deepen their knowledge of concepts in an array of contexts. This will ensure that knowledge of 'hierarchy', for example, is flexibly understood and applied to a range of literary texts.

To help to build schemas – or form a coherent web of core concepts – the teacher should be able to confidently track how a core concept is taught and, crucially, revisited through their curriculum, as in Figure 3 overleaf.

It is important to note that you cannot just keep telling students these terms and expect them to have learned how they illuminate their interpretation of literary texts. *How* you teach the concepts is important, and developing a model of subject-specific pedagogy within your team is vital to ensure that the concepts are taught well.

Remember: if you pick up a Year 8 class in an academic year, you are expecting to build upon students' prior knowledge of hierarchy in relation to the 'Great Chain of Being' in *Macbeth* when revisiting hierarchy and examining power in *Animal Farm*. The sequential nature of curriculum design such as this is incredibly useful for you to deepen students' thinking – but only if you exploit this and have a team who consistently adheres to the delivery of the spiral curriculum and utilises effective pedagogy by activating prior knowledge before introducing new material.

Below is an example of how you might do this. In this scenario, a teacher is reintroducing their Year 8 class to hierarchy as they teach students about Napoleon's rise to power in *Animal Farm*:

Class discussion questions:

1. In *Macbeth*, the Great Chain of Being established a **hierarchy**. In this **hierarchy**, who was higher up the chain: God or mankind?

Spiral curriculum and schema-building

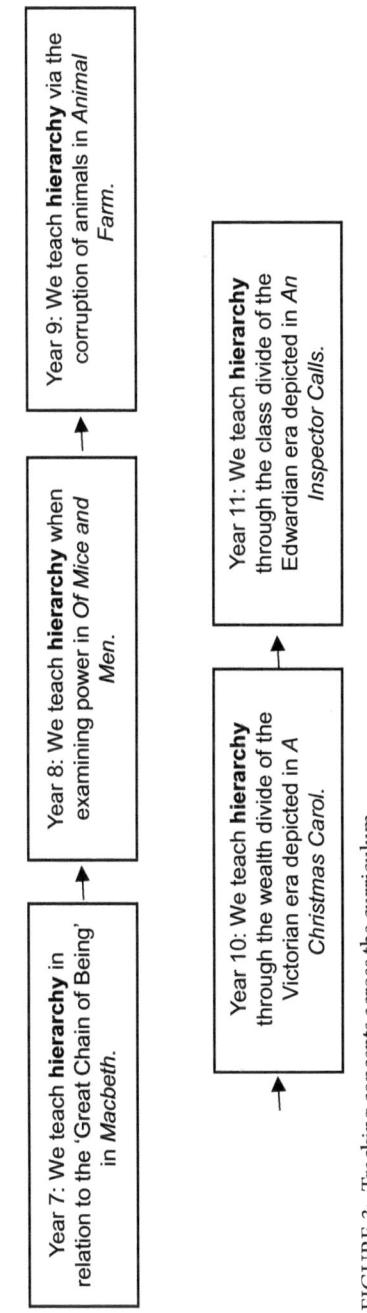

FIGURE 3: Tracking concepts across the curriculum

2. Now we know that God is the highest on the Great Chain of Being – and the Great Chain of Being established a **hierarchy**. Explain **hierarchy** in your own words.
3. In *Animal Farm*, which character is at the top of the farm's **hierarchy**?
4. Is it fair and just that Napoleon even creates a **hierarchy** on Animal Farm? Explain your answer.

… and so on.

This may seem simple – obvious, even. But with a carefully designed curriculum, all staff can do this seamlessly to build students' schemas over time. Consistently applied, this approach ensures that students make explicit links in their learning and experience your curriculum in a more meaningful way. Constantly explaining why you are teaching what you are teaching and how it links to previous learning ensures that students understand concepts far better than learning from one unit to another without making connections or drawing comparisons.

2. Disciplinary knowledge

The principles outlined above apply to this second approach, too. Instead of curriculum coherence being built around concepts, it is built around the disciplinary knowledge of English – in other words, the actions taken within a particular subject in order to gain knowledge.

For the purpose of this chapter, I will outline what I believe to be the underpinnings of disciplinary knowledge and, most importantly, how to enact these through your curriculum design.

I organise disciplinary knowledge of English into the following categories. You may have different names for these groups, but I do hope that you will recognise how these are some (if not all) of the actions that students must take in order to gain knowledge in English.

We commonly refer to these as the *Golden Threads* of a curriculum:

TABLE 4: Golden threads of a curriculum

Structures	How to construct writing at a micro (e.g. thesis statement) and macro (e.g. the discursive essay) level
Narrative	Examine how stories are constructed as both a writer and a reader
Rhetoric	The knowledge needed to debate and persuade
Genre	The conventions and tropes found in literature
Influence	The historical, social, political, religious, literary and personal factors that affect a text's production and reception
Metaphor	The ways in which we use language, imagery and symbolism to create meaning

More detail about what each of these looks like in the curriculum is given in Chapter 5.

For now, I want to illustrate the curriculum journey again, for one of the Golden Threads outlined above: **metaphor** (the ways in which we use language, imagery and symbolism to create meaning).

The concept of schema-building is important to signpost to teachers in your department here. Students should build upon prior knowledge, and revisit and develop their understanding of metaphor through the curriculum – and *how* this is taught needs to be made explicit too.

Figure 4 shows an example of how I have mapped out the teaching of metaphor across four units of work bridging Year 7 and 8, as a starting point that could be developed further into later years.

For context, here is a quick explanation of some of the key terms:

- **Tenor:** the subject of the metaphor and its intended meaning
- **Vehicle:** the language used to describe the tenor
- **Ground:** the relationship between the tenor and the vehicle.

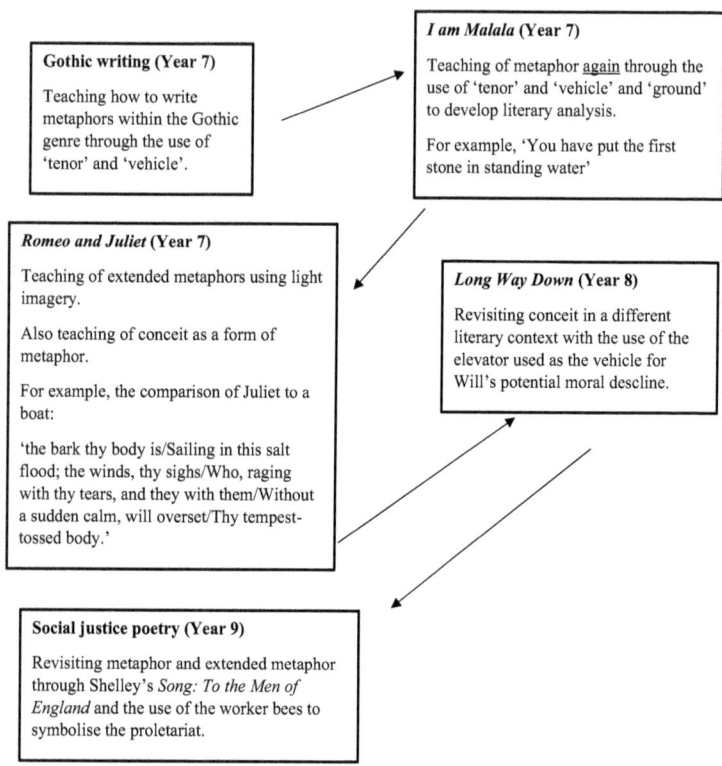

FIGURE 4: Teaching metaphor across Year 7 and 8

In much the same way as using literary concepts to build the curriculum, the purpose here is to revisit a linguistic concept in order to strengthen and deepen students' knowledge. Of course, this is the broad strokes, and lots of work is required to ensure that the teaching of metaphor is effective.

Overleaf is an example of how you might expect your team to do this. In this scenario, a teacher is introducing their Year 7 class to extended metaphor in *Romeo and Juliet*, utilising their knowledge of tenor, vehicle and ground taught earlier in the year through Gothic writing. The sequence of learning that needs to take place is described overleaf:

1. Activate students' prior knowledge of metaphor using a simple example: 'Juliet is the sun'. Ask students to explain why this is a metaphor, employing ideas from the definition in their knowledge organiser (see page 24 – a metaphor is a description of any object or action in a way that is not literally true).
2. Ask students to identify the tenor (Juliet – the object of the metaphor) and the vehicle (the sun – the language used to carry the meaning). Ensure that they justify their choice.
3. Remind students of ground (the relationship between tenor and vehicle) and use this sentence starter to ensure that students articulate this: *Shakespeare's use of the sun is an effective vehicle choice, as it depicts Juliet as…*
4. Offer students a range of other examples from the play where the vehicle choices are linked to light, such as Romeo describing Juliet as being like the sun, brighter than a torch, a jewel sparkling in the night and a bright angel among dark clouds. Explain how the metaphor is extended through these vehicle choices.
5. Ask students why Shakespeare uses a similar vehicle through each metaphor to describe Romeo's feelings towards Juliet.

In Chapter 6, I offer more detail and examples of how this might be used to develop subject-specific pedagogy within your team and what this looks like within a lesson. You should be able to see how building upon students' prior knowledge, alongside scaffolding and support, means that students deepen their knowledge of how metaphor works.

3. Explicit vocabulary instruction

Another way to build schemas is by considering how language itself works and the connections between words through very clear explicit vocabulary instruction in a spiral approach.

One approach could be drawn from Lemov et al.'s *Reading Reconsidered* (2016, p. 270), which takes 'a deep-dive into the meaning and nuances of a word in a lesson, with many opportunities for student practice'.

In any series of lessons that aim to build schemas on a grammatical level, I recommend exploring etymology, common word families, roots and affixes (morphology) because:

> 'Once students have a handle on a relatively small number of roots and affixes, they have significantly boosted their ability to accurately infer meanings of new words, as well as to deeply understand words. Knowing roots and affixes also helps students to grow attentive to a word's etymology and build a breadth of word knowledge.' (Lemov et al., 2016, p. 269)

Below is an example of how teachers might approach defining the word *wondrously*:

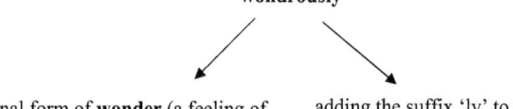

original form of **wonder** (a feeling of amazement and admiration)

adding the suffix 'ly' to the end of an adjective **turns the word into an adverb**

define : in a way that is strange, beautiful or impressive

FIGURE 5: Defining words

In this example, 'wondrously' is broken down by its root word ('wondrous') and its suffix ('ly') to show students how language is formed at a grammatical level.

Next, students can consider its usage in a text of study – in this case, the poem 'Still I Rise' by Maya Angelou, in the line:

'Into a daybreak that's wondrously clear'

Students are tasked with examining its use in the poem, before attempting to use the word in a sentence of their own to display their understanding of how the word works.

Finally, students take the acquired knowledge of how suffixes work and consider other examples of words that use the suffix to shape a word's meaning. They might do this using a 'word web', which looks like this:

Create a word web:

wondrous<u>ly</u> ⟶ strange<u>ly</u>

beautiful<u>ly</u>

impressive<u>ly</u>

_____ly

_____ly

FIGURE 6: Word web

Students make the connections between 'wondrously' and other words with the 'ly' suffix to help to build their schema regarding how language works.

Students complete an activity, similar to the above, once per week, and we carefully map which suffixes (and, later, prefixes) we explore to ensure that students continually revisit and strengthen their knowledge of language construction over time, as recommended by the spiral curriculum model.

What are the downsides to a spiral curriculum?

Critics of a spiral curriculum model often cite time as a key issue in implementation. Do teachers give enough time for mastery of key concepts or skills? This is certainly a problem in practice, but one that can be solved through a simple analogy. Imagine that you are laying the foundations of your newly purchased home. The builder informs you that there is 'not enough time' to secure the foundations; they need to erect the walls immediately. You would halt the construction process. We should not encourage learning to take place on shaky foundations if we want students to be successful.

Willingham (2010, p. 124) also poses a question that we must consider when implementing a curriculum model like this: 'Should teachers be aware that revisiting ideas can be "boring" sometimes?' Put simply: yes. That should not act as a deterrent, though. Learning, and retaining knowledge, can be perceived as a boring process, but it is a highly effective one if you are in the business of imparting knowledge that students *actually* remember and can apply in practice in future lessons.

There are countless ways to help students build schemas in the discipline of English. I have outlined three examples. You might have other methods to achieve a similar aim – and that is great. The point is that schema-building within a spiral curriculum in English is essential to deepen students understanding of the subject and to ensure that they learn in a truly meaningful way.

The case study from Amy Staniforth that concludes this chapter explores other methods to create a coherent curriculum (with schema-building at its heart). Amy is a vice principal for quality of education at a small rural secondary school. She is also the co-author of the *Ready to Teach* series and *100 for 100: Macbeth*.

Case study: Designing a secondary English curriculum

Amy Staniforth

Redesigning the English curriculum at my school has been one of the most meaningful experiences of my career. Starting with a blank slate allowed us to incorporate robust pedagogical research and create a curriculum that fosters deep learning, ensures continuity and provides equal opportunities for all students. Now, two years in, we see the results: our Key Stage 3 students are entering Key Stage 4 equipped with essential knowledge and skills that we've carefully nurtured over the years. They think about the big ideas in literature, and find it more straightforward to apply knowledge from one domain to another.

Initial reflections and theoretical underpinnings

When considering how to design the curriculum, I immersed myself in educational literature to understand different models of effective curriculum development. Books such as Mary Myatt's *Curriculum: From Gallimaufry to Coherence* (2018) and Alex Quigley's *Closing the Reading Gap* (2020) influenced my approach, but my guiding principle became the phrase 'unapologetically ambitious, unashamedly academic'. This approach informed every decision and helped to keep us focused on delivering an inclusive, rigorous curriculum.

At the outset, we focused on threshold concepts – foundational ideas that shape a discipline and open 'portals' of understanding for students. David Didau's work (2021b) was invaluable here, as he highlighted critical English concepts such as the relationship between grammar and meaning, and the effect of context on both writers and readers. Building on this, we added two of our own threshold concepts: patterns of language, imagery and plot, and the concept of power. These foundational concepts became our curriculum's backbone, informing our text choices and progression.

Identifying the problem: The 'siloed' curriculum

A siloed curriculum might be considered one where a student is taught a single topic without real-world application or connecting it naturally to other subjects in the curriculum.

In examining the typical Key Stage 3 English curriculum, I noted that it was often organised around broad topics, such as a modern novel, Shakespeare or creative writing, which students tackled as discrete units without a clear sequence. Although this format met National Curriculum requirements, it often left gaps in students' learning. Knowledge and skills were compartmentalised, meaning that students struggled to make connections between what they learned in different units, and with limited shared planning, teachers had limited awareness of students' prior learning when they advanced to the next year. Furthermore, depending on the teacher's preferences, students might experience varied texts and themes, leading to inconsistency in their literary knowledge.

A 'siloed' model, I realised, led to knowledge gaps that made it difficult for students to recall prior learning or apply their understanding in new contexts. Additionally, there was no consistent framework for text selection, which could lead to a 'diminished diet' for students. The idea of a 'diet' revolves around what we offer students through our text choices, for instance. A 'diminished diet' therefore might mean that lower-attaining classes might receive less challenging material, perpetuating inequities. Therefore, it was crucial to move away from the siloed structure and create a more cohesive, sequential model.

Building a cohesive curriculum: Big questions and thematic organisation

Our redesign centred on the concept of 'big questions': open-ended, thought-provoking questions that encapsulate core knowledge and serve as focal points for learning within each unit. We moved away from traditional learning objectives to big questions as lesson titles. For example, in a unit on power and villainy, the big question might be 'How does power corrupt?'. This approach allows students to engage with key concepts, fostering a more active, visible learning process for teachers and students.

With 'big questions' as our framework, we opted for a thematic approach, organising our curriculum around universal themes that would recur throughout Key Stage 3. This model allowed us to sequence content in a way that promoted depth and continuity, enabling students to revisit themes and ideas in increasingly complex contexts. The following themes became the pillars of our curriculum:

- knowledge and science
- friendship and coming of age
- appearance and reality
- technology and society
- love and gender

- justice
- prejudice, courage, and good versus evil
- power and villainy
- subversion and rebellion.

Each theme connected to a larger, overarching concept of power, enabling us to explore the diverse forms it takes in literature and life. These themes also allowed us to develop students' critical thinking as they examined how power shapes relationships, societies, and personal identities.

Selecting texts for breadth and depth

One of the most rewarding phases was selecting texts to represent each theme, balancing canonical works with more contemporary voices and ensuring that students encountered a wide range of genres, time periods and perspectives. Here is a sample of core texts associated with each theme:

- **Knowledge and science:** excerpts from *Frankenstein* and Phillip Pullman's adaptation for the stage
- **Friendship and coming of age:** *The Fire Eaters* by David Almond
- **Technology and society**: H. G. Wells' *The Time Machine*
- **Love and gender:** *Much Ado About Nothing* by Shakespeare
- **Justice:** *Noughts and Crosses* by Malorie Blackman
- **Prejudice, courage, and good vs evil:** *To Kill a Mockingbird* by Harper Lee
- **Power and villainy:** *Richard III* by Shakespeare
- **Subversion and rebellion:** *1984* by George Orwell

We supplemented each core text with additional materials – such as short stories, poems and non-fiction – that either supported or challenged the themes presented. For example, our unit on subversion and rebellion featured excerpts from *Fahrenheit 451* and E. M. Forster's *The Machine Stops*. The justice unit, in contrast, included historical and contemporary voices fighting for justice, such as Emmeline Pankhurst and Sojourner Truth, to highlight how literature intersects with real-world issues.

Structured knowledge and skills

Each theme was built upon a foundational set of knowledge and skills, carefully sequenced to promote mastery and provide a basis for revisiting and reinforcing key ideas. We organised our core knowledge and grammar content using a spiralled structure that ensured that students would encounter and build on core concepts year after year.

For example, in the friendship and coming of age unit, we focused on foundational narrative concepts such as bildungsroman, colloquialism and allegory, which students would then encounter and deepen in subsequent themes. Similarly, grammar instruction was spiralled, starting with basic sentence structures in Year 7 and progressing to complex syntax by Year 9. This deliberate, scaffolded approach ensured that students weren't just passively encountering concepts – they were mastering and applying them.

Assessment and ongoing development

Our curriculum also incorporated a range of assessment approaches, allowing us to track students' mastery of knowledge and skills whilst supporting their progression towards Key Stage 4. Each unit included formative assessments and opportunities for creative expression, which reinforced the thematic exploration and allowed students to demonstrate their understanding in various ways. These assessments informed our planning and allowed us to adjust the curriculum resources as needed.

Challenges and lessons learned

Launching a three-year curriculum was ambitious and it came with challenges. Implementing it across all year groups simultaneously meant that we had to support teachers as they familiarised themselves with the new structure, resources and expectations. However, seeing the impact of this work in our current Year 10 cohort – who now have a strong foundation in English and can make meaningful connections between texts and concepts – has been immensely rewarding.

The experience has underscored the importance of designing a curriculum that is both ambitious and inclusive. By providing students with equal access to challenging, high-quality literature and supporting them in making interdisciplinary connections, we are preparing them not only for academic success but also for their roles as engaged readers and thinkers. The curriculum, though a work in progress, has enriched our students' learning experiences and brought a shared sense of purpose to our teaching team.

Reflecting on the curriculum two years in, I can see areas where further refinement is needed. If I were to revise it, I would incorporate more non-fiction from diverse voices, including voices from marginalised backgrounds. I would also consider adding a verse novel, as it provides a unique medium through which students can explore language, emotion and narrative in a way that prose does not offer.

Conclusion

Redesigning the curriculum was a formidable challenge but also an invaluable opportunity to create a coherent, inclusive and rigorous programme that reflects the best of contemporary English teaching. We built a curriculum grounded in foundational concepts and structured around recurring themes and 'big questions', fostering a sense of continuity and helping students to connect their learning across years and subjects. This curriculum is designed not only to meet academic requirements but also to inspire a lifelong love of literature and critical thinking.

Chapter 5
Implementing a knowledge-rich curriculum

This chapter covers:

- definition of a knowledge-rich curriculum in English
- how to use Golden Threads to map disciplinary knowledge over time
- an illustration of how a knowledge map shapes a curriculum
- a model for a co-curricular reading programme to complement your core curriculum.

This chapter illustrates how to implement a knowledge-rich curriculum that prioritises the acquisition and retention of specific knowledge in a subject, rather than just developing skills (e.g. inference or critical thinking).

Sherrington (2018) summarises what a knowledge-rich curriculum should look like:

'In a knowledge-rich curriculum, the specifics of what we want students to learn matter and subject traditions are respected. Skills and understanding are seen as forms of knowledge and it is understood that there are no real generic skills that can be taught outside of specific knowledge domains. Acquiring powerful knowledge is seen

as an end itself; there is a belief that we are all empowered through knowing things and that this cannot be left to chance.'

I have not always taught a knowledge-rich curriculum – especially early in my career. Upon reflection, this limited how well I taught students about English as a discipline. Often, my lessons or schemes of work valued task and activity above learning content. My students did well, but this was often in spite of any thought on my part of how a curriculum can build students' knowledge of English over time.

In English, compared to other secondary subjects such as maths or science, this is much harder to achieve – in part because of differing educational philosophies held within the English teaching community, and also because of the nature of the subject itself.

This is most evident when you compare the Key Stage 3 programmes of study from the National Curriculum across the three core subjects. Table 5 is an example of how each curriculum is described. Maths and science are inherently described as knowledge-based, whereas English could easily fall into the trap that Sherrington (2018) describes as having 'generic skills that can be taught outside of specific knowledge domains'.

TABLE 5: Curriculum subject descriptions

English	Science	Maths
Reading Pupils should be taught to read critically through studying a range of authors, including at least 2 authors in depth each year.	*Gas exchange systems* Pupils should be taught the mechanism of breathing to move air in and out of the lungs, using a pressure model to explain the movement of gases, including simple measurements of lung volume.	*Number* Pupils should be taught to use integer powers and associated real roots (square, cube and higher), recognise powers of 2, 3, 4, 5 and distinguish between exact representations of roots and their decimal approximations.

(Adapted from DfE, 2014, 2015, 2021a)

The subject content is incredibly vague in English and outlines a generic view of the English curriculum as primarily skills-based.

Persuasive writing example

Let us consider how a knowledge-rich curriculum design will allow you to better specify what students need to be taught in order to do something effectively in English (more akin to the Key Stage 3 programmes of study for science and maths). In the last 15 years, there has always been an element of persuasive writing that appears at some stage of the secondary English curriculum.

When I first taught persuasive writing, I did not even consider how curriculum design could support my teaching. I fell into the trap of simply teaching persuasive writing because that appears next in the curriculum sequence. There was no consideration of how I might activate prior knowledge from previous units of work in the curriculum map (in fact, there was no map – merely siloed and disconnected schemes of work that listed tasks and activities to complete lesson by lesson) and there was certainly no suggestion of what knowledge students might require in order to write persuasively. It was, therefore, me teaching generic persuasive writing skills. And it anchored around an acronym that some of you of a particular age might remember: DAFOREST.

To clarify, this stood for:

> **D**irect address
> **A**lliteration
> **F**acts
> **O**pinion
> **R**hetorical question
> **E**motive language
> **S**tatistics
> (rule of) **T**hree

The scheme of work was essentially a series of lessons where we would read/annotate a piece of persuasive writing, identify/label DAFOREST techniques and complete extended writing on a similar topic to the reading material (e.g. the benefits of homework) using DAFOREST. And repeat.

This is not to say that there was nothing of value in these series of lessons, but there wasn't enough unpacking of each persuasive technique and the knowledge that underpins one's ability to persuade another. The other issue was that many writers whom we read, who were highly skilled in the art of persuasive writing or speaking, did *not* use DAFOREST. When it then came to students' own writing, there was a checklist approach – students felt that they had met the writing brief because they used DAFOREST, even if there was not a coherent line of argument being developed.

When I first became an English department lead, I wanted to rectify the errors of the past, so I introduced a unit of work on 'The art of rhetoric'. This was a knowledge-based unit and I felt that even the name change signposted my intentions to my team.

We began by exploring the history of rhetoric; we studied its origins from an Athenian system of democracy that relied heavily on logical debate and people's ability to solve disputes through litigation and defend their position on political issues.

Aristotle is, of course, considered the father of rhetoric, and I wanted students to consider the influence of his work on the power of persuasion. In terms of the specific knowledge that I wanted all students to have and to use, we studied Aristotle's 'three artistic proofs' in depth, namely:

- **ethos** ('character'): persuasion using the character of the speaker, identified through reputation, expertise, credibility and personality
- **pathos** ('suffering'): persuasion by appealing to the emotions, arousing sympathy, stimulating the imagination and identifying with traditions and beliefs
- **logos** ('word'): persuasion through the use of reason, respecting the role of evidence, logic, clarity and coherence.

I wanted students to know that of the three artistic proofs, Aristotle gave the most credence to *ethos*, yet understood that both *pathos* and *logos* were incredibly powerful tools with which to ensure a genuine connection with the audience.

This felt like powerful knowledge. DAFOREST was *not* powerful knowledge, and didn't offer enough context for pupils to understand how each technique achieved its aim to persuade.

Interestingly, the sequencing of the unit did mirror the DAFOREST version in parts. We did read speeches of powerful orators (Obama, Churchill, Pankhurst) in their attempts to persuade their respective audiences.

Instead of arbitrary labelling of persuasive techniques, however, we considered questions like:

- Where does Obama use logos? Why does this example offer clarity and/or coherence to his central message?
- If Churchill is attempting to validate the need for Britain to join the war effort, why is ethos necessary in this speech?
- Pankhurst's ultimatum ('Freedom or Death') is dripping with pathos. How does this impact on her audience?

We also used persuasive pieces as style models to shape students' writing. But this was different and built upon students' knowledge of rhetoric to allow them to persuade more effectively.

For example, when planning for the final piece of writing in the unit (*Write a speech persuading a person with influence to campaign for better access for girls' education across the globe*), students were not thinking about a checklist of techniques. Rather, their planning centred on ensuring that they had strong arguments for their audience, underpinned by Aristotle's artistic proofs.

Students completed a mind-map like Figure 7 to formulate their ideas for writing.

The power of utilising the knowledge of rhetoric meant that their writing was more often ideas-led rather than technique-led. Students were also more likely to understand *how* they were being persuasive, as they had a much clearer understanding of how rhetoric works. In the past, students would use alliteration, for example, and it would have no impact on the persuasiveness of their writing.

Ethos: You need to be credible, so make a list of experts you intend to cite, quote or paraphrase below:

....
....
....
....
....
....
....
....
....

Pathos: In order to appeal to emotions, outline an anecdote that you will use to highlight the plight of girls who lack education.

....
....
....
....
....
....
....
....

Logos: You need three distinct reasons to support your central argument. Outline these below:

1............................
....
....
..................................2............
....
....
....
..................................3............
....
....

Central argument: *Girls have the same right to education as boys in all countries across the globe.*

FIGURE 7: Mind map for strong argument ideas

Golden threads

If you decide that a knowledge-rich curriculum is the right curriculum model for you and your team, then the real challenge begins: what is the powerful knowledge in English that you want your teachers to teach?

A knowledge-rich curriculum needs to be carefully designed with disciplinary knowledge at the forefront of a leader's mind.

I want to remind you again of the possible Golden Threads of an English curriculum that allow us to build a map or web of knowledge that underpins a knowledge-rich curriculum.

For each Golden Thread, specific domain knowledge must be explicitly taught and sequenced carefully to build students' knowledge, and to enable them to apply this knowledge to the different curricular choices made by an English department.

TABLE 6: Golden thread knowledge

Structures	How to construct writing at a micro (e.g. thesis statement) and macro (e.g. the discursive essay) level
Narrative	Examine how stories are constructed as both a writer and a reader
Rhetoric	The knowledge needed to debate and persuade
Genre	The conventions and tropes found in literature
Influence	The historical, social, political, religious, literary and personal factors that affect a text's production and reception
Metaphor	The ways in which we use language, imagery and symbolism to create meaning

When asked about what students are studying at a particular moment of your curriculum, answering with a statement like 'we are doing *Romeo and Juliet*' reveals a lack of the thought that a knowledge-rich curriculum aimed to address. I tend to refer to text choices of topics within our curriculum as vehicles for the core knowledge that I want all students to have and be able to use.

When asked what Year 7 are studying at the end of the year, I would say something like this:

> *Our Year 7s are studying Shakespeare and gender through the vehicle of* Romeo and Juliet. *We are building upon our explicit teaching of patriarchy and agency from their study of* I am Malala *last term and refining their ability to write a piece of literary analysis. To do this, students should be showing mastery of thesis statements and use of academic verbs to write about how Shakespeare conveys ideas about gender. Academic phrases will be taught to allow students to further their practice of developing reader response.*

I appreciate that that feels long-winded. But I genuinely mean this when I say that is my response when anyone asks about my curriculum. It has to be a knowledge-rich curriculum because, as Sherrington (2018) argues, we want to ensure that 'tacit knowledge is gained, we want them to amass a body of specific declarative and procedural knowledge – not ad hoc but planned'.

The highest praise that you want as a leader responsible for curriculum design is surrounding the intention. Nothing should be left to chance. This is where the design of a knowledge map is vital.

Table 7 is an example of the knowledge map that we use at Trinity Academy Leeds, which uses similar Golden Threads to those discussed thus far. I am able to talk about our Year 7 curriculum in the way that I do because of the careful mapping of knowledge for that year.

As you read in Chapter 4, this knowledge exists within a spiral curriculum to deepen and strengthen students' knowledge over time. This is where text choices as vehicles really come into their own. In theory, you could take out a text and replace it with another and still ensure that disciplinary knowledge is explicitly taught and coherently sequenced. *Much Ado about Nothing* could easily replace *Romeo and Juliet*. Students could still learn about patriarchy and agency through either text to deepen their knowledge of these concepts.

TABLE 7: Knowledge map for Year 7

	Structures	Write like a …	Genre	Influence	Metaphor
Year 7 Terms 1 + 2: Gothic writing	**Modification:** Changing the quality of nouns or verbs using additional information, usually adjectives and adverbs **Noun:** A word that identifies or names things, animals, people, places or feelings **Verb:** A word that expresses or names physical actions (e.g. *to jump*), mental actions (e.g. *to guess*) or states of being (e.g. *to exist*) **Adjective:** A word that provides more detail or information about the noun that it is describing, usually used before nouns **Adverb:** A word that modifies a verb, telling you how, when, where or why something is being done	**Expansion:** Adding phrases or clauses to sentences to make them more complex, e.g. *Dracula, the terrifying vampire, approached me* (phrase), *Dracula was a terrifying vampire, who approached me in a sinister manner* (clause) **Phrase:** A small group of words that does not contain a verb, e.g. *the terrifying vampire* **Clause:** A group of words that contains a subject (usually the doer of the action) and a verb, e.g. *who approached me in a sinister manner*	**Dark and atmospheric settings:** Often created by spooky settings, such as dark forests or abandoned mansions **The supernatural:** Things that some people believe are real, but which are not part of nature and/or are inexplicable by the scientific laws of nature **Atmospheric dread:** A feeling of fear and foreboding		**Metaphor:** Any description of an object or action in a way that is not literally true **Tenor:** The object or action being described, e.g. *The boy was a monster* **Vehicle:** The language used to show that something is not literally true, e.g. *The boy was a monster* **Simile:** Compares two things using 'like' or 'as' **Pathetic fallacy:** Attributing (giving) human emotions or behaviour to things found in nature

Implementing a knowledge-rich curriculum 107

Leading Secondary English

	Structures	Write like a ...	Genre	Influence	Metaphor
Year 7 Terms 1 + 2: Gothic writing	**Thesis statement:** A single sentence that sets up the main idea for a paragraph of writing when studying a text **Academic verbs:** Words used to indicate what the author is doing to create meaning, e.g. *suggests, implies, describes* **Academic adjectives:** Words used to indicate how the reader might be thinking or feeling, e.g. *intrigued, mystified, disturbed, thrilled*	**Comma sandwich:** Adding a clause with a pair of commas **Three-verb sentence:** A sentence containing a list of three verbs **Two-adjective starter:** A sentence beginning with two words to describe the noun in the sentence **Extended simile:** a simile where the vehicle is described in more detail			

Year 7 Terms 3 + 4: I am Malala

Structures	Write like a ...	Genre	Influence	Metaphor
Modification: Changing the quality of nouns or verbs using additional information, usually adjectives and adverbs	**Expansion:** Adding phrases or clauses to sentences to make them more complex, e.g. *Malala, the young activist, criticised the Taliban* (phrase), *Malala was a young activist, who advocated for the right for all girls to be educated in Pakistan* (clause)	**Autobiography:** A self-written account of a person's life	**Patriarchy:** A system of society in which men hold the power	**Metaphor:** Any description of an object or action in a way that is not literally true
Noun: A word that identifies or names things, animals, people, places or feelings		**First-person narrative:** A mode of storytelling in which a storyteller recounts events from their own point of view using the first person, such as *I, us, our* and *ourselves*	**Agency:** The ability to take action or choose what action to take	**Tenor:** The object or action being described, e.g. *The boy was a monster*
Verb: A word that expresses or names physical actions (e.g. *to jump*), mental actions (e.g. *to guess*) or states of being (e.g. *to exist*)	**Phrase:** A small group of words that does not contain a verb, e.g. *the young activist*		**The Taliban:** A religious and political group that came to power in Afghanistan in the mid-1990s, known for enforcing strict Islamic law	**Vehicle:** The language used to show that something is not literally true, e.g. *The boy was a monster*
Adjective: A word that provides more detail or information about the noun that it is describing, usually used before nouns	**Clause:** A group of words that contains a subject (usually the doer of the action) and a verb, e.g. *who advocated for the right for all girls to be educated in Pakistan*	**Protagonist:** The main character, whose actions drive the plot	**Fundamentalist:** Describes a very strict, literal interpretation of a religious text or set of beliefs	
Adverb: A word that modifies a verb, telling you how, when, where or why something is being done		**Non-fiction:** Texts that are based on facts and real life, different from fiction texts, which are made up	**Inequality:** When some people lack the rights, opportunities and fair laws of others	

	Structures	Write like a ...	Genre	Influence	Metaphor
Year 7 Terms 3 + 4: *I am Malala*	**Thesis statements** and introducing authorial intent and influence **Academic verbs:** Words used to indicate what the author is doing to create meaning, e.g. *challenges, criticises, reveals* **Academic adjectives:** Words used to indicate how the reader might be thinking or feeling, e.g. *emotive, powerful, profound, inspiring*	**Comma sandwich:** Adding a clause with a pair of commas **Three-verb sentence:** A sentence containing a list of three verbs **Two-adjective starter:** A sentence beginning with two words to describe the noun in the sentence **Extended simile:** A simile where the vehicle is described in more detail			

Implementing a knowledge-rich curriculum   111

Structures	Write like a …	Genre	Influence	Metaphor
Thesis statements and introducing language exploration **Academic verbs:** Words used to indicate what the author is doing to create meaning, e.g. *challenges, criticises, reveals* **Academic phrases:** Words used to indicate how the audience might be thinking or feeling, e.g. *struck by, encouraged to, alarmed by*	**The literary present:** In literary analysis, we ALWAYS talk about the text and the writer as if they are in the present tense, even if they were writing hundreds of years ago, e.g. *Shakespeare is implying that…, The Capulets are in conflict with the Montagues…* **Modal verbs:** Verbs that show how certain your interpretation is, e.g. *this may suggest*	**Dialogue:** A conversation between two or more people **Soliloquy:** When a character speaks their thoughts aloud to themselves or to the audience **Rhyming couplet:** Two lines of the same length that rhyme and complete one thought **Foreshadowing:** Where we get hints/clues about what might happen later in the plot	**Patriarchy:** A system of society in which men hold the power **Agency:** The ability to take action or choose what action to take **Ways to talk about context:** *During the Elizabethan period…, During the 16th century…*	**Extended metaphor:** A metaphor that unfolds across multiple lines or sections of a text **Conceit:** Where the vehicle and tenor are two vastly contrasting things, and the effect is surprising, unlikely and complex **Oxymoron:** A phrase using two contrasting terms, e.g. *feather of lead* **Juxtaposition:** Two things being placed close together with contrasting effect **Symbolism:** The use of people or things to represent powerful ideas or qualities

Year 7 Terms 5 + 6: *Romeo and Juliet*

Recently, when I tentatively suggested using *Things Fall Apart* by Chinua Achebe as our vehicle text for Year 9 Terms 3 and 4, using the knowledge map (Table 7), a member of my team challenged the choice. They felt that *Purple Hibiscus* by Chimamanda Ngozi Adichie might work better. They had thought deeply about how the disciplinary knowledge that we had carefully mapped throughout Key Stage 3 could be examined through this novel in a powerful way.

My colleague argued, very convincingly, that we could use *Purple Hibiscus* because:

- One of the novel's central themes is about Kambili's lack of agency, similar to Malala Yousafzai and Juliet.
- There is the potential to widen students' understanding of fundamentalism from our study of *I am Malala*, but with a focus on Christian fundamentalism.
- There are recurring motifs (to build upon knowledge of metaphor and symbolism) with the use of flowers – the hibiscus flower in particular.
- As a writing unit, Adichie might work better as a style model – the colleague had selected passages from the novel where the opportunities to practise modification and expansion were beautiful.

So, we changed to *Purple Hibiscus*. This change was also important for the team to see from me as a leader: *my* ideas are not always the best, but *their* ideas need to fit in with the curriculum intent. In this case, my colleague demonstrated a real knowledge of our curriculum, making this a quick and easy decision. Having taught the novel using their approach, I can confirm that they were absolutely correct. Both staff and students loved it.

Breadth as well as depth

A constant tension when designing an English curriculum is the issue of breadth versus depth in what you choose for your students to learn within English.

David Didau (2018) argues:

> 'When we focus on breadth, we can introduce students to as much of our subject domains as possible. As each new aspect of our subject is introduced, students build up increasingly robust, interconnected schema.'

This is not to argue against depth. However, as with all things, there needs to be a balance. There can be a danger of a breadth approach to an English curriculum design that then means that students acquire very superficial knowledge of our subject domains. There is also the risk that we create a curriculum based solely on extracts and do not allow students to study texts in full and with the necessary depth that this entails.

When you consider the curriculum design outlined in this chapter so far, you would be forgiven for decrying its lack of breadth. So, how can you not sacrifice one for the other? How can you have both depth *and* breadth in a meaningful way within an English curriculum?

Co-curricular reading programme

Using a co-curricular reading programme, which uses one hour per week of English curriculum time, might offer a solution.

The idea is that each lesson has a quality text that has been chosen because it meets your key criteria: literary value, a broad range of voices, a range of forms and genres, appropriate level of challenge for the year group, and it compliments and enhances your English academic curriculum.

The lessons can be designed as follows:

1. **Activate prior knowledge:** Students answer a single powerful question that the teacher poses as a starting point for a discussion about the upcoming text. Questions are designed to contextualise the text and ensure that students have the necessary understanding that they need in order to access what is coming in a meaningful way. For example: *Today, we will be reading an article about families seeking justice against those who have failed them, resulting in the tragic deaths of their loved ones. What does it mean if one is 'seeking justice' against those who they think have failed them?*

2. **Reading with a ruler:** Each text is 1.5 spaced and has a wide margin so that students have space for annotations where appropriate. The teacher, as expert, reads the text out loud and students follow along, using their purple ruler. The teacher might stop every now and then to talk about elements of the text, but they also might read to the end and go back to discuss afterwards – this is down to their own judgement of what students need.

3. **Echo reading:** 'Fluent readers can read accurately, at an appropriate speed without great effort, and with appropriate stress and intonation.' (EEF, 2021, p. 19) Furthermore, Ofsted (2024) highlights that the 'broad curriculum' of increasingly challenging texts can only be comprehended through 'understanding of vocabulary, context, syntax and narrative structure, *as well as reading fluently*'. To develop this with students, they engage with a 'read aloud' task:
   a. Students listen to their teacher model reading a pre-selected passage of text (deliberately chosen to contain the words for explicit vocabulary instruction later). They might consider: *Which words are stressed? What is the pace of reading? How does the teacher pronounce certain words?*
   b. Students then practise this, either as a class (choral response) or in pairs.

4. **Summary:** Teaching summarising techniques shows students how to discern the essential ideas in a text, how to ignore irrelevant information and how to integrate the central ideas in a meaningful way. Teaching students to summarise

improves their memory for what they read and acts as a check for comprehension. Ask students the following framework questions:
a. What are the main ideas?
b. What are the crucial details necessary for supporting the main ideas?
c. What information is irrelevant or unnecessary?
d. What key words or phrases can help us to identify main points from the text?

5. **Explicit vocabulary instruction:** Our approach is drawn from Doug Lemov and colleagues' *Reading Reconsidered* (2016) and looks at the nuances of word usage. As part of this stage of the lesson, we explore etymology and common word families, roots and affixes (morphology).

For example, consider that Year 7 are studying Shakespeare and gender through *Romeo and Juliet* in Terms 5 and 6. In that unit, our enquiry questions are centred around the following concepts that underpin the 'influence' Golden Thread from our curriculum mapping:

- patriarchy
- agency
- notions of masculinity.

Our reading sources add to our students' understanding of these ideas in a highly deliberate way. The texts that students should encounter in this reading programme are highly varied, and include:

- a newspaper article from *The Guardian* (2016), entitled 'Shakespeare changed the world'
- Shakespeare's *Sonnet 18*
- Henrik Ibsen's *A Dolls House*
- 'Pyramus and Thisbe' from Ovid's *Metamorphoses* (translated by Rolfe Humphries).

This therefore allows an effort to build students' schemas more robustly through breadth, without sacrificing the depth that is valued through the knowledge mapping within our core curriculum.

Chapter 6
Subject-specific pedagogy

This chapter covers:

- how to teach writing at sentence level
- teaching metaphor through tenor, vehicle and ground
- using live modelling
- exam technique in literature essays for both GCSE and A level
- vocabulary instruction using the Frayer model.

Chapters 4 and 5 looked at the broader nature of curriculum design – the big picture thinking, the theory – whereas this chapter looks more closely at *how* the curriculum needs to be delivered by you and your team.

This chapter focuses on how those ideas can be broken down into pedagogy: what does this look like from a teacher's point of view in the classroom when the curriculum is implemented by an English teacher on the ground?

Structures

In my example of curriculum organised through pillars of disciplinary knowledge, I identified 'structures' as an action that students must take in order to gain knowledge in English. By this, I mean how to construct writing at both a micro (e.g. thesis statement or paragraph summary) and a macro (e.g. the discursive essay) level.

In the Key Stage 3 curriculum that I teach, our department has adopted a consistent approach to teaching thesis statements when students are writing literary analysis. We define a thesis statement as 'a single sentence that sums up the main idea of a paragraph'. We explicitly teach at sentence level, then move to paragraph level and eventually we apply this knowledge to writing an essay.

When we introduce students to thesis statements for the first time, in Year 7, we use a rigid syntax that students must follow:

NAME, VERB, POINT, PLACE, COMMA, QUOTATION

- NAME = the author's surname
- VERB = what the author does to create meaning, e.g. presents, depicts, highlights
- POINT = the main idea of the paragraph/line of argument being developed
- PLACE = from where in the text this main idea stems
- COMMA = used to precede embedding the QUOTATION
- QUOTATION = direct textual reference, using quotation marks.

We become flexible – and begin to break the syntax – as our curriculum develops, but this rigidity ensures that students master the key 'ingredients' that we wish them to use when constructing a thesis statement at sentence to paragraph level.

When this structure is applied, it might look like this:

> Enquiry question: *How does Stoker present Dracula as supernatural in Chapter 3?*
> Thesis statement: *Stoker [NAME] depicts [VERB] Dracula as performing supernatural actions [POINT] when spotted by Harker at night [PLACE], [COMMA] as he begins to 'crawl down the castle wall over the dreadful abyss' [QUOTATION].*

At first, this can feel contrived and restrictive. However, I always tell staff (and students) that you need to master the rules before you can break them – and we do break them. Doing so ensures that students conceptualise how to construct a line of argument, and over time, make clever choices about how best to communicate this in writing at a micro level.

Later in Year 7, when students study *Romeo and Juliet*, an enquiry question that I often teach is: *How does Shakespeare convey Romeo's shifting attitudes towards love throughout the play?*

The question style shifts from one PLACE within the text (Chapter 3) to a question that requires knowledge from multiple different moments within the text (shifting attitudes throughout the play). This means that a different syntax to our thesis statement might produce a stronger response. This time, we teach our students to use the following order, tweaked from earlier in the curriculum model:

PLACE, COMMA, NAME, VERB, POINT, QUOTATION

We also build students' competency in writing literary analysis by writing multiple paragraphs to track character development.

> Paragraph 1: *Prior to meeting Juliet [PLACE], [COMMA] Shakespeare [NAME] conveys [VERB] love as a source of pain for Romeo [POINT] when describing it as a 'choking gall' [QUOTATION].*
>
> Paragraph 2: *Upon meeting Juliet [PLACE], [COMMA] Shakespeare [NAME] highlights [VERB] a clear shift in Romeo's joyful expression of love for Juliet [POINT] by saying that 'Juliet is the sun' [QUOTATION].*

These subtle changes over time demonstrate a progression and very carefully track how students' written literary analysis develops. Simply by positioning PLACE at the beginning of a thesis statement, students show a greater awareness of the author's craft and, in particular, are able to comment on the structural patterns of a text.

Of course, when students enter Key Stage 4, their literary analysis should be much stronger and less reliant upon a particular structure. All good scaffolding fades over time.

Our approach to teaching the structures that underpin interpretations in literature changes, but it is firmly built upon the strong foundations of the Key Stage 3 curriculum.

For example, when introducing students to *An Inspector Calls* and essay technique, we explicitly show students how we have progressed from Key Stage 3 to Key Stage 4.

Imagine that students are preparing for an assessment early in the GCSE course on this text. The question that students will answer is: *How far does Priestley present Birling as a man who only cares for himself and his family?*

The following is the guidance that we give students in terms of the micro and macro structures of answering a discursive essay:

> *When writing about a character from* An Inspector Calls, *it is important that you consider their journey throughout the play, their characterisation and how they act as a vehicle (or metaphor) for Priestley's ideas.*

Note that the reference to *vehicle* builds upon students' prior knowledge of metaphor from the Key Stage 3 curriculum.

How to write an introduction

For any question, there are three things to cover in your opening paragraph:

1. All the characters are constructs that serve a function.
2. How, related to the question?
3. The text warns, challenges, subverts, attacks or critiques as relevant to the question.

Then they provide a model example of how this works with the sample question.

> (1) Priestley presents Birling as a man who only cares for himself and his family, and is therefore used as a dramatic vehicle representing the capitalist greed of many factory owners in pre-war Britain. (2) Caring for only himself and his family drives a selfishness caused by his desire to accumulate wealth and improve his social standing. (3) In this, Priestley attacks those who care about themselves and do not take responsibility for improving the lives of all members of society.

Like our approach to thesis statements, there is a structure to the introduction, but it is more about the guiding principles of an effective introduction than a rigid structure that must be adhered to.

When we teach the main body of the essay, this is where our prior knowledge of thesis statements feeds into the macro structure of the essay.

We remind students that in Years 7 to 9 we insisted that they always used the following syntax (order) for a thesis statement:

NAME, VERB, POINT, PLACE, COMMA, QUOTATION

It is important to then exemplify what that looks like when applied to answering a question about *An Inspector Calls*.

TABLE 8: Syntax for thesis statements

NAME	Priestley
VERB	(immediately) establishes
POINT	Birling as the physical representation of capitalist greed
PLACE	in the opening stage directions
COMMA	,
QUOTATION	describing him as 'heavy looking'.

This becomes:

Priestley immediately establishes Birling as the physical representation of capitalist greed in the opening stage directions, describing him as 'heavy looking'.

This works, but we want students to think and write more flexibly now. We allow them to break the syntax and experiment with it, but keep the ingredients that make it effective in establishing a line of argument.

We tell students that they require a range of thesis statements across the essay to clearly demarcate and build on their arguments in relation to the question, in well-defined paragraphs.

Now that they are in Year 10, we encourage students to be more flexible with the syntax of their thesis statements. However, the key ingredients are the same for what we might call our *topic sentences*. This a subtle shift from thesis statements, where students choose any appropriate order for the ingredients, rather than being restricted to a singular set order. For instance, students might lead with PLACE or POINT.

TABLE 9: Syntax for thesis statements

NAME	Priestley
PLACE	, in the opening stage directions,
VERB	describes
QUOTATION	him as 'heavy looking'
COMMA	,
POINT	which immediately establishes him as the physical representation of capitalist greed.

So this then becomes:

Priestley, in the opening stage directions, describes him as 'heavy looking', which immediately establishes him as the physical representation of capitalist greed.

Over time, students may choose to write autonomously when setting up their main ideas, but they will have learned and embedded the above model, which will have helped them to construct flowing sentences effectively.

As a leader, your job is to ensure that your team all rows in the same direction with a pedagogical choice such as this. Staff may be resistant, but they need to understand that this has been built upon the curriculum, across different teachers, and so the coherence must take precedence above what an individual teacher wants to do. Side before self, always.

Metaphor

Earlier, the approach to teaching metaphor was to build knowledge of tenor, vehicle and ground cumulatively over time.

Here is an example of how it might influence the pedagogy of teachers within your department if implemented consistently.

First, a brief recap of the following terms:

- **tenor:** the object or action being described through metaphor
- **vehicle:** the language used to carry the meaning of the metaphor
- **ground:** the relationship between the tenor and the vehicle.

Consider the metaphor 'Juliet is the sun'.

The tenor is Juliet, as she is the object being described by Romeo. The vehicle is Shakespeare's choice to compare her to the sun. She is, of course, not literally the sun; therefore, Romeo is speaking metaphorically. The ground, essentially, is where students explore Shakespeare's language choice, i.e. why is Juliet similar to the sun?

Perhaps because she juxtaposes the darkness of mood that consumed Romeo whilst in the throes of Rosaline's unrequited love? Of course, you may have other interpretations.

Many might argue that students do not *need* to know parts of metaphor to understand what Romeo is implying here. However, we need to think more cumulatively about students' acquisition of knowledge. If students understand how metaphors actually work, fundamentally, then this sets them up for far greater success in their study of English over time.

Below is an example of a lesson towards the end of an academic year, explicitly teaching metaphor. This approach, enabled students to understand metaphor beyond the superficial meaning and illustrates why I feel that you should utilise a knowledge-rich approach to teach English.

For context, students were working on sentence construction in the 'grammar for writing' unit that complements our study of *Macbeth*. They were presented with a picture prompt as their focus and asked, akin to David Didau's slow writing approach (2012) (to get students to slow down and approach each word, sentence and paragraph with love and attention), to use a simile start to write the opening sentence of a description of a medieval soldier engaged in battle.

Throughout the year, I frequently reminded students that simile is a type of metaphor and that too often students rely on using animals as the vehicle, e.g. *Like a lion, the soldier was fierce in battle.*

One of my students actually wrote this, before scribbling it out when they remembered the 'no animal as vehicle' rule!

It is amazing how often they want to use animals to describe the tenor (in this case, the soldier/soldier's sense of bravery) and they really struggle when I say, 'You cannot use an animal as your vehicle.' They groan, but it gets them to think harder about how metaphors work.

For instance, with the student's answer above, I enquired why they had chosen 'lion' as their vehicle. They rather eloquently explained:

If the soldier is the tenor, I want to choose a vehicle that shows that they are like a really fierce warrior. That was the ground I was trying to create there. And lions are fierce, so it works, but then I forgot you always say no animals.

The student had clearly grasped how metaphor works, despite their upset that they had used 'lion' as a vehicle against my rule. I would certainly argue that knowledge of these terms led them to be far more conscious of how they craft metaphor, which should benefit their analysis of how other authors use metaphor in their work too.

The next step was to change their vehicle, so we discussed how we could achieve the same ground but change the vehicle. The question to the class became: *What vehicle could be used to show that the soldier is a fierce warrior?* The answers ranged from 'Vikings' to a student's mother (I will not go into the context of that!) to a storm.

In the end, the class decided on 'storm' as a better choice than 'lion' and crafted a simile start with this new vehicle. The Year 7 student wrote:

Like a storm, the soldier raged through the battlefield to seek out their foe.

What was interesting was the removal of 'fierce' in this redrafted sentence, which we then analysed as a class in terms of their language choice. It was felt that the word 'fierce' was not needed, as the use of 'storm' presented a more effective vehicle with which to imply the intended ground. In other words, the student was 'showing, not telling'.

Another student summarised this perfectly:

If the vehicle is chosen well for the tenor, the ground implies something without being too obvious. The storm is fierce – and raging – just like the soldier in battle, I suppose. It works.

If we want students, therefore, to analyse metaphor, we should really offer the knowledge of parts of metaphor to help students to truly understand them.

Live modelling

I still remember one of the most difficult questions that I was given at interview for an English leadership post:

We all know that modelling is essential in teaching, but what does good modelling look like in English?

I still think about this a lot. Most of us will give an articulate answer as to the benefits of modelling, but when this is asked about specifically within a subject (*in English*), it becomes much more complex. It is even more complex when you want your department to deliver consistent, high-quality modelling in the classroom.

As a leader, you need to set the standard, establish the mental model and support your team in achieving your goals.

As I have progressed through my career, I have improved my approach to modelling. I have also observed modelling in English that too often involves students being presented with a model answer, followed by students spending time examining its strengths and areas for development. In the best-case scenario, this is teacher-led, where an expert highlights strengths and weaknesses to students (who do not possess the same level of expertise), and in the worst-case scenario, students are left to work this out for themselves.

It's similar to when you first began your teaching career and were asked to observe a brilliant teacher do something with which you were struggling. For example, if you were struggling with behaviour, you might have observed an experienced colleague with a class whose behaviour was remarkably calm and absent from low-level disruption.

However, merely *watching* this without an explanation of the steps that the teacher took to get to this seemingly idyllic state just leaves you feeling bad about yourself. You are likely to then believe that the teacher is simply great at behaviour because of *who they are* – which is rarely the case. I always liken this to when a student teacher observes a lesson where behaviour is exemplary and assumes that the behaviour of the class is just good, when, in reality, the graft of the teacher and the subtle, more tacit strategies that they are using go unnoticed.

I wrote a chapter in *Cognitive Apprenticeship: In Action* (Tomsett, 2021) about how unhelpful it is to hand out model writing without dissecting the author's successful techniques as a group. Put simply, students are unlikely to make use of potential models of good writing acquired through reading because they don't yet understand *how* authors produced such text. Therefore, live modelling is the optimal approach to unearth the complex thought processes that contribute to, say, discursive essay writing.

Here is the method that I ask my department to use when engaging in live modelling. You can also use this when live-modelling the writing process for a creative task.

Most of you will be aware of the 'I do, we do, you do' approach and will likely implement some form of this within your practice – whether across a single lesson or a series of lessons. In case you are unfamiliar with this practice, or need a reminder, here is a useful definition:

In the broadest sense, the 'I do, we do, you do' model involves an expert teacher carefully sequencing a series of steps, starting with explicit or direct instruction, which ultimately leads to students working independently.

As an English teacher, I most commonly adopt this approach for extended writing tasks or essay writing.

I do

In the *I do* stage, as I explore in further detail in my chapter in *Cognitive Apprenticeship: In Action* (Tomsett, 2021), I use live modelling as the best 'model of instruction that works to make thinking visible' (Collins et al., 1991, p. 6).

For an example, see the script and commentary in Figure 8, where I model how to write an introduction to the question based on the GCSE set text *An Inspector Calls* by J. B. Priestley: *How far does Priestley present Mrs Birling as an unlikeable character?*

Commentary	Writing
_____ = using tentative phrasing to create a sense of debate	Whilst Mrs Birling is seemingly an unlikeable character, Priestley presents her as more complex than that.
• focusing on her attitude based on class system	Although she shows contempt towards the working classes and adopts a sense of superiority over others based on class, she is merely a (product) of the Edwardian class
contextual linking / influence of society	system.

FIGURE 8: Model introduction plan

The commentary column acts as thinking prompts, making the expert thought processes explicit to the learners. This is supplemented with verbal explanation.

We do

In the *we do* stage, the teacher helps their students by providing scaffolds such as prompts or partially completed sentence stems.

For this, I use a commentary alongside the live modelling itself, where I explicitly write down what I am thinking at each stage of writing, to elicit success criteria whilst providing prompts to aid students' writing.

For example, students may only be given the commentary first, and then asked to replicate the introduction on Mrs Birling using this alone, with my live model example removed from students' view.

Here, scaffolding guides students, without being excessive.

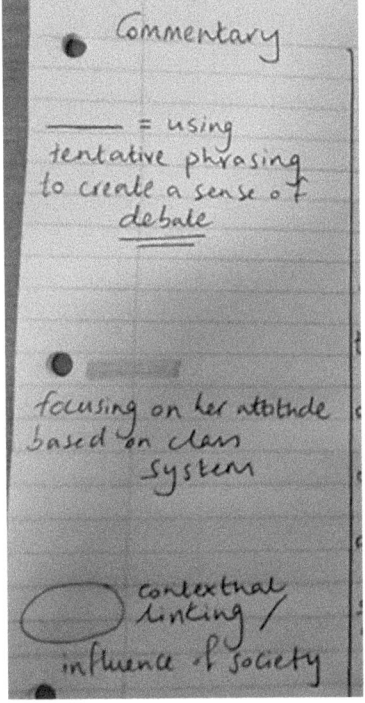

FIGURE 9: Introduction prompts

You do

Finally, in the *you do* stage, students follow the steps to show their understanding on their own. To do this, I want students to have understood the procedural knowledge required to construct an effective introduction, so I ask them to replicate what has gone before by writing both a commentary *and* the introduction, using a similar grid approach to the *I do* stage.

To ensure that we move beyond emulation, this time the students do this with a slightly altered question, which will draw from their domain knowledge of the text in a different capacity.

Students might answer: *How far does Priestley present Mr Birling as an unlikeable character?* Teachers can then assess how well students have met the success criteria elicited earlier in the process, but evaluate how this has been shaped towards different content from the text of study.

How can we tell if students truly understand the process and can apply it to another context?

I do this by expecting another *I do* stage, but this time based on a completely different text from students' study of literature. I pose this task:

> *Write an effective introduction to the question 'To what extent are we sympathetic to Scrooge in* A Christmas Carol?*'*

Now here is where we see what the students have learned about the thinking process that underpins the writing explicitly modelled by the teacher. The new question asks the student to carry out the same task to formulate a response, but has flipped the statement and changed the character.

Our success criteria will need to be shaped in order to meet the requirements of this new task, perhaps to something like this:

- Use tentative phrasing to establish a sense of debate.
- Focus on Scrooge's attitude towards others.
- Consider the influence of society on characterisation.

Whilst this is the same for the most part, the ability to refocus the thinking to a different context is the challenge. The real test for the student is: Can I write as effectively in this task as I did in the previous task? If not, why not? What is stopping me?

The answer to those questions will then allow me to evaluate my teaching approach, and thus the cycle continues, where I am back to *I do* if necessary.

Exam technique

I firmly believe that a consistent approach to exam technique – both for GCSE English and A level English – is a sure-fire way to ensure effective outcomes for all students and from all teachers in your department.

In the following section, I suggest a few different ways you can create a uniform approach to exam technique, either to implement in your department or to galvanise your thinking about how you might do something similar within the context of your English department.

GCSE

GCSE English exams inevitably shape a teacher's pedagogy. They should also, then, shape a *department's* pedagogy. I believe that there should be consistency across *how* exam technique is taught.

Planning for a GCSE English literature extract question

On the surface, the extract appears to be a gift for students – they have a section of the text with which to engage, and no quotation recall is necessary – but here are the obstacles that I find that students stumble over:

- spending a long time trying to decode the language employed by Shakespeare in the extract
- focusing on words that they do not know, rather than on what they do know
- relying heavily – or sometimes solely – on the extract and not developing a wider range of ideas.

I have implemented what I refer to as the 'crossing-out method' with a couple of English departments to much success and to combat these stumbling blocks.

Teachers in your department will guide their students through the following steps:

1. Identify where the extract comes from in relation to the narrative of the play, e.g. Act 3, the climax, the turning point.
2. Ignore the extract initially and jump straight to the question to identify the question focus, e.g. aggressive male behaviour.
3. Highlight lines that students feel are relevant to this focus.
4. Then, crucially, cross out anything that has not been highlighted.

How is this different from merely highlighting key information, then?

- It is a cathartic experience that illustrates to students that you cannot (and nor should one attempt to) write about everything.
- It reduces cognitive load in terms of decoding difficult language, whilst also teaching students the need to judiciously select relevant information.

Figure 10 demonstrates how this might look

I have highlighted lines from the extract that refer to the two central ideas (1 and 2), and the rest is not needed to answer this question.

As a class, we then discuss what we look at specifically in relation to that line, with a quick bullet-point list:

1. R blames his love for J for making him 'effeminate', which affects his masculine traits of aggression using 'valour's steel'.
2. Metaphor – willing aggression into his very being to give him strength to kill T.

The last piece of the puzzle is modelling how we write about the rest of the text – *beyond the extract*.

I like to keep this simple and add ideas to our bullet-point list, drawing from students' knowledge of the text. As a rule of thumb, I suggest that they aim for up to five ideas for any given question, so in this particular example, we would need three more.

This is what I pop up on the screen:

Romeo and Juliet – final assessment
Read this extract from Act 3, Scene 1 of *Romeo and Juliet* and answer the question that follows. At this point in the play, Romeo has discovered that Mercutio is dead and Tybalt returns. Romeo fights Tybalt. [FP1]

> **MERCUTIO**
> ~~Help me into some house, Benvolio,~~
> ~~Or I shall faint. A plague o' both your houses!~~ ⟵ Climax, turning point
> ~~They have made worms' meat of me. I have it,~~
> ~~And soundly too. Your houses!~~
> ~~*Exeunt* **MERCUTIO** *and* **BENVOLIO**~~
> **ROMEO**
> 5 ~~This gentleman, the Prince's near ally,~~
> ~~My very friend, hath got his mortal hurt~~
> ~~In my behalf. My reputation stained~~
> ~~With Tybalt's slander—Tybalt, that an hour~~
> ~~Hath been my kinsman!~~ O sweet Juliet,
> 10 Thy beauty hath made me effeminate   1.
> And in my temper softened valor's steel!
> ~~*Enter* **BENVOLIO**~~
> **BENVOLIO**
> ~~O Romeo, Romeo, brave Mercutio is dead!~~
> ~~That gallant spirit hath aspired the clouds,~~
> ~~Which too untimely here did scorn the earth.~~
> **ROMEO**
> 15 ~~This day's black fate on more days doth depend.~~
> ~~This but begins the woe others must end.~~
> ~~*Enter* **TYBALT**~~
> **BENVOLIO**
> ~~Here comes the furious Tybalt back again.~~
> **ROMEO**
> ~~Alive in triumph—and Mercutio slain!~~
> ~~Away to heaven, respective lenity,~~
> 20 And fire-eyed fury be my conduct now.   2.
> ~~Now, Tybalt, take the "villain" back again~~
> ~~That late thou gavest me, for Mercutio's soul~~
> ~~Is but a little way above our heads,~~
> ~~Staying for thine to keep him company.~~
> 25 ~~Either thou or I, or both, must go with him.~~
> **TYBALT**
> ~~Thou, wretched boy, that didst consort him here~~
> ~~Shalt with him hence.~~
> **ROMEO**
> 28 ~~This shall determine that.~~
> ~~*They fight.* **TYBALT** *falls*~~

Starting with this extract, explore how Shakespeare presents aggressive men in the play.
Write about:
- How Shakespeare presents aggressive men in this extract.
- How Shakespeare presents aggressive men in the play as a whole.

[30 marks]
AO4 [4 marks]

FIGURE 10: The crossing-out method

1. R blames his love for J for making him 'effeminate', which affects his masculine traits of using 'valour's steel' – more aggressive than he's been.

2. Metaphor – willing aggression into his very being to give him strength to kill T.
3. ?
4. ?
5. ?

In the earliest stage of teaching this approach, teachers should live-model and script their thinking processes. Then move on to guided practice, before fading scaffolding to the point where students can tackle this independently.

This might seem laborious at first, but it is all about longer-term gains. If we model the thinking process effectively at the planning stage, students will eventually write better essays.

A level

There are some overlaps between GCSE and A level, and you might find the principles interesting to apply there if you stick with reading.

The following example is specific to a particular question type at A level that appears commonly across all the examination boards.

> *To what extent do you agree that…?*

At A level (and GCSE too, of course), students lose far too many marks for not answering the question in full and considering all its constituent parts. How often have you or colleagues in your department cried aloud in frustration, 'Why can't they just answer the bloody question?'. It happens.

Specifically with the example of *To what extent do you agree that…?*, this is due to ignoring what I refer to as the 'hinge' words or phrases that allow students to do two vital things:

1. engage critically with the question (and, therefore, fully address the question requirements)
2. develop a genuinely cogent argument.

A 'hinge' word or phrase is the element of the question that helps to 'open up' a sense of debate and allows you to develop a clear line of argument. I use this metaphor and it seems to stick.

To identify how this works in practice, consider this A level English literature question below:

> *'In* The Kite Runner, *resistance against those who have power and influence never succeeds.' To what extent do you agree with this view?*

The hinge phrase (in this case) is: *never succeeds*. This is important to highlight to students very clearly, as the question is not merely asking students to consider 'resistance against those who have power and influence'. They are being asked to *evaluate* whether this 'never succeeds' and build an argument around that view.

The A level literature course is filled with these question types, and the hinge approach applies to them all:

- *'The principal focus of the novel is on the personal suffering of the female characters, rather than the repressive power of Gilead.' To what extent do you agree with this view?*
- *'In* The Kite Runner, *Hosseini is more interested in oppressors than in their victims.' To what extent do you agree with this view of the novel?*
- *'In the worlds that Atwood presents, men are always oppressors.' To what extent do you agree with this view of the novel?*

To examine how the hinge approach works further, now consider this question:

> *'In the worlds that Atwood presents, men are always oppressors.' To what extent do you agree with this view of the novel?*

Ensuring that your department (and, your students) understand the difference between an essay where you write about men being oppressors in *The Handmaid's Tale* and an essay where you argue whether they are always oppressors will be the difference in the grades that students achieve at A level.

This is because often you might have teachers in your department who are incredibly knowledgeable about a text but less so about the exam technique required when writing about that text in an exam. This tacit knowledge needs to be effectively taught to students; as the leader of an English department, you need to ensure that this happens in all classrooms.

Let's take this further, consider the different scenarios that might arise when students write their introductory paragraphs – their thesis – where they establish a key line of argument; this is vital in securing the higher grades at A level.

For Students A and B, carefully consider which student is actually addressing the question requirements or, in other words, which student utilises the hinge of the question.

Student A

In Atwood's novel, men are clearly the oppressors of women concerning their fertility, autonomy and self-determination within a brutal totalitarian theocracy. The systematic oppression of the Gilead residents appears through the corrupt religious laws enforced by men. This is perhaps typified through the society's requirement of Handmaids to participate in the Ceremony, an unjust procreative ritual, which is, in essence, a form of rape in disguise – a symbolic representation of oppression in itself, through an act of a male penetrating a woman.

> **Student B**
>
> *Whilst undoubtedly the men are the principal oppressors of women within Gileadean society, whether they are always the oppressors is questionable. The systematic oppression of the Gilead residents appears through the corrupt religious laws, which are certainly enforced by men but are also propagated by more powerful women such as the 'Wives' and 'Aunts'. This is perhaps typified through the society's requirement of Handmaids to participate in the Ceremony, an unjust procreative ritual, where the wife is equally culpable for the rape of the Handmaids. So, whilst men are primarily the oppressors, they are not always responsible for all acts of oppression in the novel.*

Student A's introduction engages with the ideas from the question, but it does not develop an argument. One of the key differences between GCSE and A level literature, however, is that just engaging with the text is not enough – students must develop a cogent argument. The hinge approach might prove useful in achieving that aim.

Student B makes explicit references to their own argument being developed (e.g. men are primarily the oppressors, but not the only oppressors). This makes for a more thoughtful and developed response than that from Student A, who is merely engaging with the key words from the question.

Vocabulary instruction

I have written about vocabulary instruction, in relation to curriculum design (see page 89), but it is also worth providing an example to illustrate English-specific pedagogy with a strategy that many schools use on a whole-school level.

You might have heard or seen others use the Frayer model as a method of explicit vocabulary instruction. It is a visual grid that helps students to understand and organise new vocabulary, and can be a highly effective vocabulary learning tool in your department.

The Frayer model looks like this:

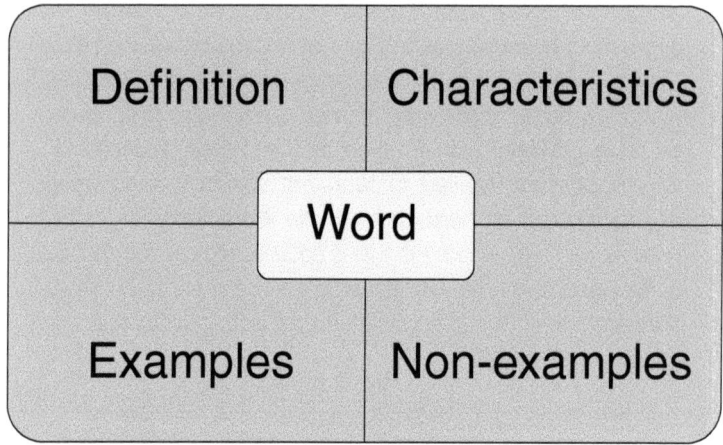

FIGURE 11: The Frayer model for vocabulary learning

Use it for introducing:

- linguistic methods
- structural methods
- word choices that contain figurative ideas, to unpack their meaning.

In this instance, I want to demonstrate how you might use it when introducing oxymorons to your students. Oxymorons are likely to appear within your curriculum at various stages (think Romeo's famous 'O loving hate' or Byron's 'melancholy merriment' in *Don Juan*, or even Auden's 'juicy bone' referred to in 'Funeral Blues').

The Frayer model is useful for debunking student misconceptions, such as what truly constitutes an oxymoron. The 'non-example' section helps to eliminate words or terms that aren't defined as an oxymoron. I find that the 'non-example' is too often overlooked by many English teachers/departments. Many teachers and students see the non-example as anything that isn't the example, which diminishes its pedagogical purpose of helping to identify or clarify the words or terms that might appear ambiguous at first but which do not fall into the definition.

When my department used the Frayer model to introduce oxymorons to Year 7, we began by examining 'non-examples' first:

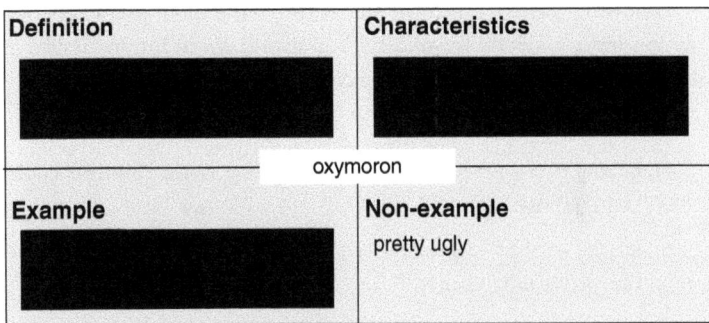

FIGURE 12: Frayer model non-examples

We discussed what the phrase *pretty ugly* meant. This began at a literal level, where students zoomed in on 'ugly', and then evolved into a discussion of being 'quite' ugly. Eventually, we got students to think about syntax and the contrasting nature of the two words (although students often got there first!). We then revealed the 'example':

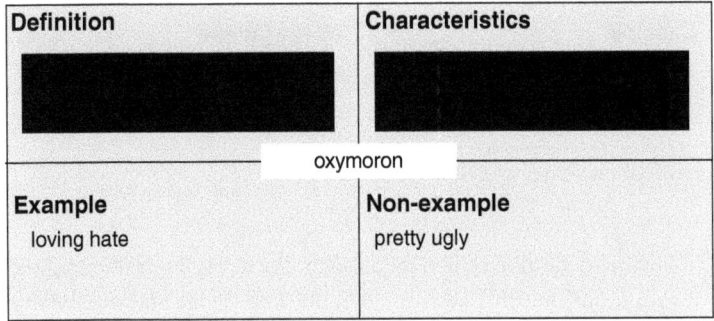

FIGURE 13: Frayer model example

Students then considered why 'loving hate' is an oxymoron but 'pretty ugly' is not. Some struggled and thought that both were opposite words side by side, before remembering – or being told – that 'pretty', in this context, is not the opposite to 'ugly', which opened up a discussion about the context of language choices, and which then developed a greater appreciation of vocabulary.

Following this, we asked the students to write their 'characteristics' section independently to solidify (but also to check for any issues in their understanding of) how the oxymoron works.

Year 7s in our department came up with:

- *having two different ideas near each other* (close, but this could be juxtaposition)
- *having two opposites next to each other* (closer, but could fall into the 'pretty ugly' trap)
- *sort of two things, maybe like opposites, beside each other* (better, but not firmly understood perhaps).

The next reveal:

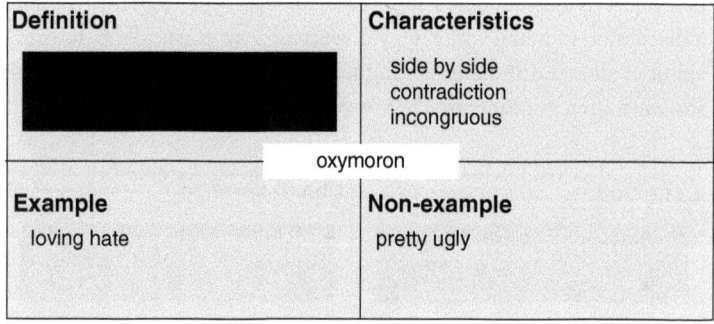

FIGURE 14: Frayer model characteristics

Further definition is then required for the terms 'contradiction' and 'incongruous', but this adds to students' knowledge and vocabulary, which is essential. Students need to understand the concept of the term to have any chance of understanding authorial intent beyond just spotting the term in texts.

Finally, we reveal our working definition, which we expect all students to use in its exact form, due to all the work that we have done so far to get to this point.

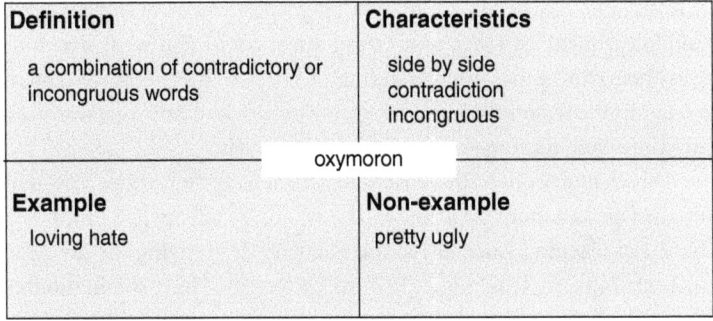

FIGURE 15: Frayer model full working definition

In my experience, this is often where I see English departments stop using the Frayer model. It almost becomes a de-contextualised activity, isolated from the rest of the curriculum and students' next stage of learning. This should not happen.

What students should do next is to analyse the use of an oxymoron in another text in your curriculum model. For us, this was a short extract from *Don Juan*, and we explored Byron's 'melancholy merriment' in relation to this stanza:

It is an awful topic—but 't is not
My cue for any time to be terrific:
For checker'd as is seen our human lot
With good, and bad, and worse, alike prolific
Of melancholy merriment, to quote
Too much of one sort would be soporific;—
Without, or with, offence to friends or foes,
I sketch your world exactly as it goes.

Whilst challenging, and obviously requiring further instruction of the poem's central ideas, contextual influences and so on, the students deftly evaluated the use of oxymoron. One student began their analytical paragraph:

> *The speaker presents a rather incongruous idea, by presenting the seemingly contradictory 'melancholy' with 'merriment' in relation to their view of the world...*

The student has begun to analyse language choices of 'melancholy' and 'merriment' in a way that I think most could. But what struck us was their conceptual understanding of the definition that we crafted earlier in the lesson through the Frayer model, and how this was used to inform and illuminate their language analysis.

This chapter ends with a case study from Grace Johnston, a head of English and assistant principal at The Albion Academy in Salford. She has been teaching since 2018, and is currently studying for her MSc in Learning and Teaching at Oxford University. Here, she highlights the importance of consistency across the department with teaching literary analysis through her 'Why that method?' approach.

Case study: The importance of consistency

Grace Johnston

If there's one thing that I've learned in my time as a head of department, it is the importance of consistency. When I first took on the role of head of English at my school (at the time, an incredibly challenging secondary school in a very deprived area of Salford, with poor results as a consequence of historically low expectations), almost all the teachers in the department were teaching the subject in different ways. There was little, if any, cohesion when it came to subject-specific pedagogy; from class to class, students experienced almost entirely different versions of the curriculum, depending on their teacher.

It therefore became one of my top priorities to create alignment and regularity in both what we taught our students and how we taught it. That isn't to say that I – or anyone else in the department – was aiming for exact uniformity. One of the great joys of teaching (especially a subject like English) is that it can be so distinctive to the individual teacher and so informed by our personal passions, interests and ways of thinking. However, I firmly believe that establishing an element of consistency in subject-specific pedagogy is a springboard for the success of a department.

One of the best examples that I have of the benefits of establishing consistency in subject-specific pedagogy is the 'Why that method?' scaffolding sheets that my amazing lead practitioner drafted, and which we refined and rolled out together (available to download for free on my website missjohnston.com). To outline the initial problem: when it came to analysing the impact of methods, we found that students in different classes were wording their analyses completely differently and with varying levels of accuracy, specificity and success. Some were using beautifully precise analytical language; some were merely inferring under the guise of analysing; others were utilising lovely vocabulary but not necessarily thinking carefully about the *specific* impact of a particular method (there are only so many times you can read 'The writer uses [insert literally any linguistic or structural method here] to evoke an image of…' before your brain starts to go numb!). Some teachers were using a set bank of phrases during their modelling of analysis; some were changing their phrasing from one lesson to the next; others were spending valuable lesson time debating the most effective phrasing (when this wasn't part of the main learning intention). The teaching of method analysis in our department was just not efficient or effective.

We therefore invested our time and energy into crafting our 'Why that method?' sheets, which are now a staple in English lessons across our whole department. They have been remarkable for our teaching of analysis and for the success of students' responses. First and foremost, establishing consistency in this aspect of our pedagogy reduced cognitive load for both staff and students. Teachers no longer have to waste precious lesson time debating how to word the impact of a method – we just choose the most relevant phrase from the sheet and craft an effective sentence based on this key vocabulary. Meanwhile, students are also more able to utilise their valuable working memory to understand the precise impact of *this* particular method in *this* particular context. If we already know that repetition 'creates a continual reminder' of something, then we can invest more time in carefully considering exactly what the writer is creating a continual reminder of and why. If we know that caesura can 'create an unexpected pause to symbolise an abrupt end or accentuate a pertinent message', then we can invest more time in debating what this symbolism or pertinent message might be. In other words, providing consistency in the *phrasing* of our analysis has allowed students to flourish in their *actual analysis*. Not only does consistency of this kind support cognitive load, but it also sets an agreed standard for the quality of students' work. Yes, this is something that takes time and effort, but – like with most things – it pays off in the product: students' knowledge and skills, and their ability to showcase these through their writing.

However, almost as important as the product – the consistency in approach – is the route that you take to get there. Deciding on agreed approaches to subject-specific pedagogy is an incredibly enriching and team-building experience for a department. If you foster a culture of embracing debate and passion in the discourse surrounding your subject and its pedagogy, it can cultivate a department-wide attitude of commitment to and enjoyment of continuous development in your subject knowledge. Our 'Why that method?' sheets are not something that I created myself in isolation and then insisted that the whole department used – that, I'm sure, would have gone down like a lead balloon. These sheets are something that we developed *together*. They are something that we have refined and developed continuously together over time. We have revisited, amended and added to the phrasing of them over the past couple of years. Some of my colleagues will frequently stop me excitedly on the corridor and say things like '10L2 have come up with another potential impact of a semantic field!', and then we'll discuss, refine and add it to our document. Thus, I think that it's important to think carefully about the aspects of pedagogy in which you want to create consistency. Not only should they be grounded in educational research, your own and others' expertise and your experience of what works, but you should also make sure that they are a focus of discussion within your department. Consistency for the sake of consistency is futile – we need to create consistency in the things that really matter and are truly impactful, and we need to ensure that our teams understand and are invested in the 'why' as well as the 'what' and 'how'.

Chapter 7
Assessing using curriculum-related expectations

This chapter covers:

- the purpose and rationale of assessment in English
- what we mean by curriculum-related expectations (CREs)
- how assessment using CREs provides better feedback about curriculum delivery.

Before I explain how you might implement curriculum-related expectations (CREs) as an assessment model in your department, it might be pertinent to reflect on the purpose of assessment in English itself more broadly.

Clare Sealy (2020) poses two 'golden' questions to ask ourselves as the leader of a curriculum in order to determine its effectiveness:

1. 'What do we want to find out?
2. What are we going to do differently as a result?

This chapter argues that CREs are a much better alternative to what has dominated assessment practices in English in the past.

The old days

Depending on your age, and when you began your teaching career, you may or may not remember National Curriculum levels. For those who are unaware, they were a set of eight bands, established by the government and used to measure a child's progress against other pupils of the same age across the country. The levels applied to children in Key Stage 1, Key Stage 2 and Key Stage 3.

Each National Curriculum level was also divided into sub-levels:

- C meant that a child was working at the lower end of the level.
- B meant that a child was working comfortably at that level.
- A meant that a child was working at the top end of the level.

TABLE 10: Key Stage assessment levels pre-2014

SATs	KS1*	KS2	KS3
Level 1			
Level 2	Expected		
Level 3			
Level 4		Expected	
Level 5			
Level 6			Expected
Level 7			
Level 8			

*Assessed by the teacher (rather than external examiner)

To support teachers assessing students in English, we used APP (Assessing Pupil Progress). If you are unfamiliar, this was a structured approach to periodic assessment, developed in the late 2000s and used in schools in England and Wales. It aimed to help teachers to use diagnostic information to track student progress and to identify strengths and weaknesses based on specific assessment foci (AFs). APP was designed to be used consistently across the National Curriculum. For instance, there were seven AFs for reading that described the key elements of performance in this attainment target, linked to the National Curriculum programmes of study. The level descriptions were designed to give a detailed view of pupils' attainment across all the key stages and in all types of reading.

These also existed for writing, speaking and listening. I will illustrate with reading, and you will get the idea…

TABLE 11: Assessment foci for reading

AF1	Use a range of strategies including accurate decoding of text, to read for meaning.
AF2	Understand, describe, select or retrieve information, events or ideas from texts and use quotation and reference to text.
AF3	Deduce, infer or interpret information, events or ideas from texts.
AF4	Identify and comment on the structure and organisation of texts, including grammatical and presentational features at text level.
AF5	Explain and comment on writers' uses of language, including grammatical and literary features at word and sentence level.
AF6	Identify and comment on writers' purposes and viewpoints and the overall effect of the text on the reader.
AF7	Relate texts to their social, cultural and historical contexts and literary traditions.

This was used to assess reading proficiency for English at Key Stage 3. In principle, it makes sense, and some of the language above still existed in mark schemes at GCSE.

There are, however, some problems with this skills-based approach to English assessment.

Let's explore this with AF5 and consider what a Level 6 student should 'do' versus a Level 7 or Level 8 student.

Level 6: *Across a range of reading*:

- Some detailed explanation, with appropriate terminology, of how language is used.
- Some drawing together of comments on how the writer's language choices contribute to the overall effect on the reader.

Level 7: *Across a range of reading*:

- Comments begin to develop precise, perceptive analysis of how language is used.
- Some appreciation of how the writer's language choices contribute to the overall effect on the reader.

Level 8: *Across a range of reading:*

- Clear appreciation and understanding of how the language used supports the writer's purpose and contributes to meaning.

Confusing? Absolutely. Pretty much the same as GCSE assessment? Absolutely. Supports you in gauging how well a student knows and has understood your beautifully sequenced curriculum? Absolutely not.

In 2014, these levels were scrapped. We cheered, we applauded, we celebrated... and then most English leaders panicked. What would assessment look like in Key Stage 3 English?

Most decided that it would be GCSE-lite assessments, which were subject to the same pitfalls of APP. Many may also argue that students should do a similar reading and/or writing task to the GCSE. I have witnessed countless examples of assessments in English that do this very thing:

- *Write a story about a character who makes a strong impression.*
- *Read the extract below. How does the writer use language to describe Napoleon?*
- *Write a description as suggested by this picture.*

I am not saying that there is no merit in asking students these questions, but I would argue that Key Stage 3 does not have to wholly mirror Key Stage 4 English in our approach to assessment.

When you consider a mark scheme that you might create for your department, would it really be any different from APP or GCSE mark schemes? I do not imagine that it would be.

You can't do much to change the constraints of GCSE assessment in English in your role, but this does not need to infect Key Stage 3. We are all guilty of using the assessment itself in GCSE English language to teach it. But how many in your team bemoan this? How many in your team do this because *there is no other way*? I would argue that using CREs is a much better alternative.

When you consider the issues that arise each year with exam marking from the GCSE papers, across all exam boards, they provide clear evidence that this assessment approach does not tell you as a curriculum leader how well your students have learned *your* curriculum.

In fact, rather shockingly, according to Ofqual (2018, p. 4):

> 'The probability of receiving the "definitive" qualification grade varies by qualification and subject, from 0.96 (a mathematics qualification) to 0.52 (an English language and literature qualification).'

We do not need to fall into the same trap with a beautifully designed Key Stage 3 curriculum. Far too often, assessment practices at Key Stage 3 do not directly assess specific knowledge taught in the curriculum. This is a problem.

So we return to another approach at Key Stage 3: CREs.

With the generic, GCSE-lite assessments at Key Stage 3 as outlined previously, I do not believe that you will find out much beyond the superficial:

- *Students struggled to understand the extract.*
- *Students paraphrased quotations, rather than analysing them meaningfully.*
- *Students relied on word-level analysis, but could not connect the ideas to the author's intent.*
- *Students' spelling, punctuation and grammar were relatively weak.*
- *Students did not quite understand what 'make a strong impression' meant when writing about character.*

Overall, the assessment did not reveal much about the enaction of curriculum across your department. It probably was not that useful, relative to the demands of marking, for you to be able to interrogate your curriculum from that dataset alone.

In other words, can you confidently lead any changes that you want to make to the curriculum and/or pedagogy for your whole team?

What do you do differently as a result? It can be a minefield in this form of assessment.

Curriculum-related expectations (CREs)

Let's look more closely at what you can do differently as a result of your assessment, as this links with the power of CREs as tools with which to quality-assure your curriculum model.

Cast your mind back a moment to the previous chapters in Part two. I need you to imagine the efforts that go into your role in developing a thoughtfully planned, well-sequenced and coherent knowledge-rich curriculum. Without an assessment model that reflects back how well students have learned *that* curriculum, things begin to fall apart for you and your team. CREs are a much better tool with which to quality-assure your curriculum delivery. In essence, CREs are a set of knowledge and skills that students are expected to demonstrate by the end of each school year/term/key stage.

CREs help you to specify (Chapters 4 and 5), teach (Chapter 6) and assess (this chapter) the knowledge that we expect the students to be taught by all members of your department. Your assessment model should check – at a very granular level – whether your students have learned what you have explicitly taught them.

Stephen Rollett (2019) summarises this well:

'This requires us to have a keener understanding of the granular components of the curriculum and an awareness of how these build together into composites of knowledge and skill.'

The granular components of the curriculum might come from your mapping of knowledge. For example, if I know that students have learned the following from the Golden Thread of **metaphor** in my curriculum design by the time they get to studying Jason Reynold's *Long Way Down*, I need to check whether they can show off *this* knowledge in assessment conditions.

TABLE 12: Key terms for understanding metaphor

Metaphor	Any description of an object or action in a way that is not literally true
Tenor	The object or action being described through metaphor
Vehicle	The language used to carry the meaning of the metaphor
Ground	The relationship between the tenor and the vehicle
Conceit	A metaphor where the tenor and vehicle vastly contrast and the effect is unlikely, surprising or complex

The questions that I write for my team to check students' understanding in relation to the text they are studying, need to help us to track what students do or do not know from the curriculum, and what they can or cannot do from the curriculum. This will allow you as a leader to decide what your team might do differently, to help with future curriculum mapping.

Here is one example to illustrate the approach.

Long Way Down is a verse novel following the aftermath of a shooting, in which the narrator, 15-year-old Will, struggles to come to terms with the death of his older brother, Shawn. In a poem towards the beginning of the novel, entitled 'The Sadness', Will expresses his sadness by using an analogy to compare the loss of his brother to a tooth being aggressively ripped from his mouth:

I could set an open-ended question, such as: *How does Reynolds use language here to convey Will's feelings?*

However, if my curriculum has explicitly taught parts of metaphor and conceit, I want to gently nudge/direct my students to mention metaphor or conceit in their answer. Students could, of course, answer this question without utilising any knowledge explicitly taught in the curriculum mapping, but then what purpose does that serve? And if, when left to their own devices, students only do a superficial word-level analysis, how do I know that my curriculum is really making a difference to students' learning?

Students, in the absence of CREs, may well make comments like:

> *Reynolds is saying that Will is incredibly sad because he describes losing his brother as 'the worst part'. He reinforces this with the word 'absolute' to show that Will is completely grief-stricken.*

Except… that is not what Reynolds is doing. He is using the conceit of comparing a tooth being ripped out of one's mouth to the inexorable grief that one faces when losing a loved one. This concept all lies within the use of metaphor.

In the example above, the student hints at what the tenor is (*losing his brother, Will is completely grief-stricken*) but does not examine why it is an effective vehicle choice in this conceit, nor examine the ground to really draw out the ideas from Reynolds' beautiful use of language.

If asked about it more intentionally, students may do this more (and even if they do not, you can plan to do something about it in future teaching).

Using CREs, I might ask the following questions to begin:

1. Briefly state the **tenor** of Reynolds' **conceit** in the poem 'The Sadness'.
2. Identify three relevant **vehicle** choices matched to the **tenor**.
3. Explain, in a single sentence, the **ground** (the relationship between tenor and vehicle).

I do this to check for the application of knowledge from the curriculum. The questions are sequenced in such a way as to check whether students truly understand how metaphor works (*what* the author is describing, *how* they are describing it and *why* they are describing it in this way).

Following this, students will need to practise applying the knowledge in extended writing, using the **structures** Golden Thread that I explained in the previous chapter with the use of **thesis statements**.

Again, check at a granular level that students can use thesis statements rather than launching into an essay, where a whole cohort of students will have tackled the generic nature of the question in a myriad of ways, leaving you as a curriculum leader with very little to dissect in terms of how well the curriculum has been taught by your team.

4. Write a **thesis statement** in answer to the question: *How does Reynolds use language to convey Will's feelings?*

   This is to ensure that students are setting up their line of argument well. It might be (as you discover with the final question) that students can explore language choices but cannot tie it all together.

5. How does Reynolds use a **conceit** to convey Will's feelings in the poem 'The Sadness'?

The idea is that students will then apply their knowledge to a piece of extended writing. Below is an example of what a Year 8 student wrote in response to this question, having successfully answered questions 1 to 4.

> *Reynolds skilfully uses a conceit to convey the emotional suffering that Will faces having lost Shawn, describing how grief is similar to how someone 'rips' a tooth out. This image of a violent ripping of the tooth from the gum reflects precisely how Will feels: like his brother has been ripped from his life, leading to pain and anguish at this loss. This is further reinforced by the image of a tongue 'constantly slipping' into the 'empty space' where the tooth was. The 'empty space' might symbolise Will's loss, and 'constantly slipping' perhaps implies that this loss cannot be forgotten; it is a constant reminder of the grief that Will feels. Finally, when a tooth is ripped out, it does not grow back, which is what has happened to Shawn. He has been murdered and will not return to Will, therefore making this conceit convey the permanence of both loss and pain that Will feels now and always will.*

There are a few things to observe in this answer:

1. Thesis statement

The student uses the syntax explicitly taught, with a slight tweak. They added the adverb 'skilfully'. This was something that we discussed as a word that could be added to a thesis statement, and the student has adopted this within their academic register.

2. The absence of 'tenor', 'vehicle' and 'ground'

There is no requirement for students to use this vocabulary in their answer. This is because this is part of a teacher's pedagogy, and whilst it is made explicit in questions 1 to 4, it becomes part of the implicit writing process in extended writing.

This does not happen immediately. Initially, students often use the language itself until the understanding of how metaphor works becomes more implicit. For example, another student wrote the following during their literary analysis of Reynolds' conceit:

> Reynolds uses the vehicle of a 'ripped tooth' to convey the pain and suffering Will feels after his brother is killed.

There is nothing wrong with this, but it can become clunky, and I often tell my department that the move from explicit to implicit analysis of metaphor should be the goal for students.

3. Other grammatical structures

If a member of my current department read the answer that I have provided, they would recognise other grammatical structures that we explicitly teach through our curriculum. For example, *the image of* is a stock phrase that we ask students to use when exploring an author's language choices, to avoid needless and distracting comments like *The verb 'ripping' suggests…* or *The abstract noun 'empty space' implies…*, which do not add anything to students' analysis.

We also teach students to use tentative phrasing, so the use (and arguably over-use!) of modal verbs (*might, may, perhaps*) stems from this.

Finally, the phrase *this is further reinforced by* is also explicitly taught as a method with which to build upon a previous idea, so many of our students will incorporate this into their writing.

Once more, I am not advocating that you must ask your department to teach in this particular way, but having an agreed pedagogical approach that complements your curriculum model is more likely to ensure that students make progress throughout the English curriculum, without students having to switch to a different teacher's method or style each year as they progress through secondary school.

The curriculum as a progression model

The ultimate aim of using CREs is to ensure that the beautiful curriculum that you have designed for – or alongside – your team acts as a progression model, rather than age-related expectations or generic skill-based criteria. In essence, students make progress if they are learning your curriculum and can do more as a result of your team's delivery of that curriculum.

David Didau summarises this, stating that the curriculum as the progression model simply means that 'we make judgements of progress based on how much of the curriculum a child has learned' (Didau, 2021a).

Didau expands upon this to then consider the power that lies behind such a view of curriculum and assessment. He states:

> 'Having curriculum related expectations helps us to specify, teach and assess the knowledge we expect children to acquire. It becomes reasonable to expect all students to have met these expectations because they are – or should be – directly connected to what has been taught.' (Didau, 2021a)

Michael Fordham (2017) reinforces this idea when he explains that 'This is why the curriculum is the progression model: if a student has learnt the curriculum, they have made progress.'

Like many things in education, it sounds simple, but the implementation of CREs in order to use the curriculum as a progression model is far more complex.

Do you have the curriculum coherence to use CREs? In other words, does your curriculum have logical skill and knowledge progression? For example, if you are teaching students to use modification (changing the quality of nouns and verbs), do students have the prerequisite knowledge of word classes and also the opportunity to apply this knowledge flexibly over time in a range of contexts?

But if you consider *how* students are assessed in GCSE English, it does not lend itself to working backwards and specifying what knowledge students should be taught and how best to sequence this to enable progress over time.

Consider what a student must evidence to achieve a Level 6 (the highest level in the mark scheme) in AQA's GCSE English literature:

TABLE 13: Assessment objectives for GCSE

AO	Typical feature
AO1	• Critical, exploratory, conceptualised response to task and whole text • Judicious use of precise references to support interpretation(s)
AO2	• Analysis of writer's methods with subject terminology used judiciously • Exploration of effects of writer's methods to create meanings
AO3	• Exploration of ideas/perspectives/contextual factors shown by specific, detailed links between context/text/task

One might infer from this that students ought to know how metaphor works for AO2 ('writer's methods'), but if a curriculum model is driven by what texts you teach, and as a leader you do not specify to your team exactly what we mean by *metaphor* and how metaphors work, or sequentially teach metaphor from the simple usage to the more complex usage, it is likely to be a random, scattered approach to teaching metaphor prior to beginning the GCSE course.

This feels like a lost opportunity and does not account for the students' learning journey across five years of study.

An interesting thought experiment to stress-test your curriculum coherence is to hypothetically move schemes or units of works around to different terms or years. Would it actually make a difference?

In my example earlier of sequencing the teaching of metaphor, it would make a huge difference. If Year 8 students studying *Long Way Down* were going to analyse the use of conceit, consider their journey up to that moment.

In Year 7, students are taught simple metaphors during their study of Gothic writing. My department uses *His blood ran cold* as an example of a classic metaphor. The tenor (*blood*) and vehicle *(ran cold)* are easily identifiable. We explicitly teach that the ground is *conveying fear*, to build students' knowledge of how metaphor works.

In their next unit of work, students revisit metaphor in their study of *I am Malala*. This time, we consider how tenor is often implied in metaphor (that is, it cannot merely be identifiable through the quotation, as it can be in *His blood ran cold*.)

We all teach the same metaphor from the autobiography:

'*"You have put the first stone in standing water", they said. "Now we will have the courage to speak".*'

Most students recognise the vehicle of *put[ting] the first stone in standing water*, as it is clear that this is not meant literally. However, the tenor implied is *Malala's rebellion against the tyrannical Taliban*. This is more difficult to understand but is vital, as often the tenor in metaphor is implied. This then allows students to consider the ground in the metaphor and to make links to rebellion and the stone disturbing the standing water, and the subsequent analysis of symbolism that this allows.

At the end of Year 7, students' knowledge of metaphor is built upon with the introduction of extended metaphor (of light – *Juliet is the sun, She doth teach the torches to burn bright, bright angel*) and conceit (Capulet compares Juliet to a boat in a storm and extends the metaphor, comparing her eyes to a sea, her tears to a storm, her sighs to the stormy winds and her body to a boat in a storm) when students are taught *Romeo and Juliet*.

Therefore, when students reach their assessment section on *Long Way Down*, the questions below (as we saw earlier), feel like a natural progression through the curriculum:

1. Briefly state the **tenor** of Reynolds' **conceit** in the poem 'The Sadness'.
2. Identify three relevant **vehicle** choices matched to the **tenor**.
3. Explain, in a single sentence, the **ground** (the relationship between tenor and vehicle).
4. Write a **thesis statement** in answer to the question: *How does Reynolds use language to convey Will's feelings?*
5. How does Reynolds use a conceit to convey Will's feelings in the poem 'The Sadness'?

Unless you specify that this knowledge should be taught throughout your curriculum and then, as a leader, ensure that it is delivered by your team, this assessment approach does not work. Specificity and careful sequencing are absolutely crucial.

As is too often tragically true in our education system, the more advantaged students will do well despite a lack of curriculum coherence or an assessment model that checks what is taught in the curriculum in a granular way – although that is not to say that you must only use such an approach in schools with a higher percentage of disadvantaged students.

As a leader, how do I best use this assessment data?

The beauty of this assessment system is that you can, as a leader, have a firm understanding of the following post-assessment:

- Which students know more from your curriculum?
- Which students can remember more from your curriculum?
- Which students can do more from your curriculum?

Imagine that you are in a situation post-assessment where you used the assessment objectives (AOs) in Table 14:

TABLE 14: Assessment objectives

AO	Typical feature
AO1	• Critical, exploratory, conceptualised response to task and whole text • Judicious use of precise references to support interpretation(s)
AO2	• Analysis of writer's methods with subject terminology used judiciously • Exploration of effects of writer's methods to create meanings
AO3	• Exploration of ideas/perspectives/contextual factors shown by specific, detailed links between context/text/task

You are conducting analysis of students' performance at a class level to consider how well students have done in a recent assessment or exam with the different teachers within your team.

Class A

Students achieved between Level 3 and Level 4 on average. This indicates that students were able to:

- show a clear understanding of the task
- use textual references to support a range of comments
- clearly explain the effects of the writer's methods
- clearly understand ideas/perspectives/contextual factors.

Class B

Most students achieved a Level 5, with a few students achieving a Level 6. This indicates that students were able to:

- show a thoughtful understanding of the task
- use apt references integrated into interpretation(s)
- examine the effects of the writer's methods
- thoughtfully consider ideas/perspectives/contextual factors.

I appreciate that you might conduct an analysis like the above. I believe that introducing CREs would make this analysis far more specific.

The language used here is typical of GCSE exam board mark schemes, yet you cannot advise a member of your team that they need to ensure that students *examine* rather than *clearly explain* the effect of the writer's methods and expect this to actually mean anything.

The other difference between Class A and Class B here is semantics, centred around the word *thoughtful*. This is so open to interpretation that using this as the vehicle with which to drive improvements in your team's students feels laughable.

Consider an alternative that evaluates what has been taught explicitly in the curriculum and its success thus far. It utilises the Golden Threads from curriculum design and what is contained within the knowledge mapping to be very precise in terms of what students did well, and it identifies areas of improvement.

Class A

TABLE 15: Student assessment

	What went well	Areas for development
Structures	Students used the correct syntax of a thesis statement.	However, the POINT (e.g. Will's suffering in grief) and QUOTATION did not suitably link. This meant that students did not develop a line of argument in their paragraph.
Metaphor	Students explored language choices and explored the vehicle choices when addressing metaphor.	However, students did not explain the ground well, which meant that they did not connect the language ('the empty space') with the meaning (the void in Will's life now).
Influence	Students explained the implicit idea of emotional pain resulting from death as a permanent loss (using the idea of the tooth not growing back, for example).	

Class B

TABLE 16: Student assessment

	What went well	Areas for development
Structures	Students used the correct syntax of a thesis statement, where the POINT and QUOTATION were closely matched. This meant that students could develop a clear line of argument in their paragraph.	
Metaphor	Students demonstrated excellent knowledge of Reynolds' use of a conceit.	However, there were missed opportunities to consider layers of meaning by using 'This is further reinforced by' sentence stems within a paragraph.
Influence	Students considered the wider contextual factors of Will's grief (as a result of the cyclical nature of gun violence in his neighbourhood, for example).	However, they often failed to match this back to the use of the conceit. Only one student linked the violent description of a tooth being ripped out with gang violence, for instance.

This offers a greater insight into the curriculum delivery by your team for the students they teach. It is easy for you as a leader to know *why* a class has achieved a mark in an assessment in a meaningful way.

The teacher of Class A will need to revisit thesis statements (good news, though – it comes up again and again in a spiral curriculum!) and explicitly reteach the relationship between POINT and QUOTATION.

The teacher of Class B can provide a feedback lesson with a specific focus on layering analysis, using *This is further reinforced by* to ensure that students develop their exploration of different vehicle choices within a metaphor.

The most salient advantage of using CREs is that the feedback needed for each individual class becomes self-evident *because* of the assessment design and its incredibly close mirroring to curriculum design.

Reporting

I have deliberately not mentioned the reporting process that underpins any formal assessment until now. Reporting is a difficult one to get right, as parents and carers have a limited understanding of how assessment is conducted in schools. It is, of course, necessary to report assessment data to parents, and you are likely to be at the behest of a whole-school system as to what this looks like in your context.

For me, when using CREs, the simplest system is to convert marks into an overall percentage score and report that. There will of course be someone with a much greater knowledge of how to do this than me who can think about ways in which this could then be converted into a progress score (e.g. *working towards, on target, above target*, etc.) rather than an attainment score.

However, as a leader, it is important that you deal with data sensitively with and on behalf of your team. It is a hard balance sometimes, especially in schools where data appears to drive *everything* that happens within the subject.

If we return to the fictitious Class A and Class B, you will notice that I gave no indication of numerical attainment. Nor did I provide context of students' prior attainment (or 'ability' if you use that word, although I much prefer to consider the prior attainment of students rather than notions of ability, which can be perceived as fixed in some way) within the classes.

Students will have a range of different starting points in your school, and if, Class A was entirely comprised of high-prior-attaining students and Class B was a class of low-prior-attainment students, comparing the average percentage score of each class is pointless. Saying that 'On average, Class A achieved 85 per cent, whereas Class B only achieved 57 per cent, indicating Class A are performing significantly better' is not helpful for the students taught by members of your team.

If we consider the purpose of assessment from a student's perspective, it should inform students of the following:

- Where am I now?
- Where am I going?
- How am I going to get there?

Therefore, the feedback that teachers provide to students, in order to close knowledge gaps identified through an assessment, is all that they really need to concern themselves with.

As a leader, though, you might want to ensure that students are indeed making progress through the curriculum. However, there are certain things that data can and cannot do to support you in this.

Most importantly, know that any analysis that you do choose to do with internal data should be focused on how different students, classes or year groups have performed *on one particular assessment in a snapshot of time*, but not on comparing the results of *different assessments from different times*. Failure to do so might lead you on a wild goose chase, in an attempt to close gaps in your curriculum that is not needed.

As discussed countlessly throughout the course of this book, having a clear mental model of what you want assessments to do for you, your team and others is needed. This needs to be communicated clearly and shared with all, so that everyone understands what assessment reporting looks like for you in English.

Table 17 is an example of how to communicate with different stakeholders when reporting on assessment:

TABLE 17: Reporting on assessment

Relevant stakeholder	How data from assessments is communicated
Students	This should come in the form of feedback delivered by the teacher. It should specifically address areas for improvement from the assessment, linked to the curriculum map, and teachers must offer the opportunity for students to act upon the feedback given. *AFI: You need to ensure that the QUOTATION in your **thesis statement** helps to support your POINT. Complete the task below to practise...*
Teachers	Teachers should compare the results of their class with those of another class in the same year group where prior attainment banding is similar. This will allow them to compare AFIs and seek advice or support from that teacher or the head of department in order to address the delivery of this curriculum area. *My class scored an average of 72 per cent; a class of students with similar prior attainment scored 85 per cent. When I looked at their exam scripts, I noticed that language exploration was stronger. I will speak to that teacher about how they taught **ground** this term.*
Head of English	The head of English needs a snapshot of how all classes have performed in order to identify any potential under-performance of classes. *In Year 7, all classes bar one were able to identify the differences between **tenor** and **vehicle** when examining metaphors. Class X really struggled, so I need to have a conversation about how Year 7 teachers are delivering this part of the curriculum.*
Parents/ carers	Parents and carers are likely to understand raw percentage scores that show how well their child has learned the curriculum. When reporting assessment data, this must be contextualised to ensure that parents know how well their child has performed relative to their starting point. The report card will look like this:

	Joe Blogg's English score	Class average %	Year 7 average %
	45%	32%	60%

*AFI refers to Area for Improvement

I am certainly not the only leader using CREs as a robust assessment method for secondary English, as the next case study from Kirsty Pole demonstrates. Kirsty is in her 14th year of teaching and is currently head of English at an 11–18 school in Leicestershire. Prior to this, she has held roles as lead practitioner of English and head of year. Most importantly, she has pioneered the use of CREs in her department, and this is her journey to making that decision.

Case study: Why curriculum-related expectations?

Kirsty Pole

Since I joined my school in 2018, we've been on a journey – sorry, we do all love an education-based buzzword, don't we? When I joined the school as a lead practitioner and new member of staff, I was teaching texts that I'd never taught before and I spent most of that first year planning my lessons from scratch. There was a loose scheme of work on a Word document and lots of resources in a folder on the shared area, but I spent a lot of time planning and sharing in that first year. I realised pretty quickly that every member of the department was planning and delivering similar lessons, but there wasn't a collaborative sharing culture and we couldn't be sure that pupils were being taught the same things at the same time unless we verbally discussed it. As a communicative department, we knew that we were all teaching similar things at similar rates, but there was a lack of consistency and no set expectations for what pupils should know and what pupils should be able to do by the end of our topics.

Fast-forward to the present day and I'm now head of English at that same school. I've always believed in autonomy in the English classroom; every class teacher knows their pupils best, so who better to decide what is taught, when and how? But consistency is just as important, ensuring that every pupil is getting the same quality of lesson and is being taught the same essential knowledge and skills needed to succeed. At GCSE and A level, success is measured in outcomes, but at Key Stage 3 there are no nationwide assessments anymore, and since the removal of levels in 2014, secondary schools have been left to their own devices when it comes to how to assess progress. The default for English departments when it comes to assessment is often to use GCSE-style extended writing at the end of a topic, but there are two major issues with that model:

1. Year 7 isn't GCSE, so why are we assessing them in the same way?
2. Doing one piece of extended writing at the end of a topic and then using it as an example of pupils' progress is flawed in many ways.

Oftentimes, when asked 'why do you do it like this?', the answer is 'Because we've always done it like that' – which is never a good reason to do anything. So, as a department, we have been focusing our attention on two things since 2023: Key Stage 3 curriculum and Key Stage 3 assessment.

Curriculum-related expectations and assessment

The first thing that we did was to reduce the number of topics that we teach at Key Stage 3. Key Stage 3 curricula are often cluttered, but there is no need to do six topics in an academic year just because they fit nicely into each half-term, and frequently they don't end up fitting nicely into the half-terms anyway – they end up running over, or teachers find themselves trying to cram the reading of a novel into lessons to the detriment of pupils' understanding. Giving more time to each topic allows teachers to ensure that they aren't only teaching content but that they have time to teach skills as well.

Secondly, as a department, we decided that each topic would be resourced in the following way:

- a booklet
- a set of basic PowerPoint lessons
- curriculum-related expectations
- a knowledge organiser.

All of our classes are mixed ability, from Year 7 to Year 11, so it was important that all of our curriculum decisions were made as a team; we needed buy-in from everyone to ensure consistency, so we made all the decisions together.

Once we had our topics in place, the work moved to assessment. There were two things that we needed to decide:

1. What do we need to learn from the assessments that we give?
2. What do the pupils need to learn from the assessments that we give?

We knew that we wanted to move away from the extended writing at the end of a topic, instead opting to build more opportunities for extended writing into lessons, with the support of a teacher. We also wanted summative assessments to focus on assessing pupils' knowledge of the topic and their skills in writing about it. So often with secondary English assessment, we feel the need to assess our Key Stage 3 pupils in the same way as our Key Stages 4 and 5, without considering that the curriculum itself can be a progress model alongside regular formative assessment.

After reading David Didau's blogs about the work that he was doing at OAT (Ormiston Academies Trust), we decided to trial using curriculum-related expectations for each topic. We chose:

- a list of ten key terms for the unit, which pupils would need to be able to define
- a list of what pupils know
- a list of what pupils can do.

These were to become our success criteria for each topic. Our assessments would be built around assessing what pupils know and what pupils can do. I am lucky to work with a collaborative team, and we decided the CREs together for each topic; I genuinely believe that this is essential to their success. We were all committing to them; we were saying that you could walk into any classroom on our corridor and see us teaching the same knowledge and the same skills to our classes. The same applies to the booklet and the PowerPoint slides that form the resources for each unit. Each member of staff took responsibility for planning a topic, and the booklet and PowerPoint slides are available as a foundation for the classroom teacher to build on; this was a way of ensuring consistency for pupils without removing a teacher's autonomy. We then created a version of the CREs for pupils, which they have in their exercise books, and we refer to these throughout our topics, highlighting to pupils what knowledge they are learning or what skills they are practising.

Our next challenge was to create summative assessments that would allow us to see the impact of the CREs. You only have to scroll through X (formerly known as Twitter) to see that assessment at Key Stage 3 is a topic of constant discussion – how to do it, whether we are doing it right, whether there actually is a right or wrong way – and it's a discussion that we had as a department (and still do), many times. However, the CREs enabled us to develop a new way in which to assess progress – our assessments are based on the CREs. After all, this is what we have agreed to teach students, and shouldn't we be assessing what we've taught? The main point of assessment is to find out how successful we have been at implementing our curriculum, and if the assessment outcomes are poor, we need to review our approach to implementation.

After researching and speaking to other English teachers and leaders, we decided to trial a new assessment model that would assess what pupils knew and what they could do, without the need for unsupported extended writing assessments. Assessments would be carried out three times a year and would assess what pupils had studied over a term. We relied on examples generously shared from David Didau at Ormiston Academies Trust and Donal Hale at Trinity Academies Trust, and crafted our own versions of these assessments. We trialled our first assessments in 2023–24, and feedback from the English team was positive: staff felt that they assessed both knowledge and skills, and we were able to obtain the information from them that we needed as teachers in order to accurately understand how well we'd taught the curriculum. However, in our department discussions, we also considered the importance of formative assessment in deciding a pupil's progress, and how often in secondary education it seems to be overlooked. Alongside our CREs, we decided on methods of formative assessment that we would use every lesson to assess whether students are mastering the content that we are teaching them. Some of the methods on our list include:

- retrieval practice
- mini-whiteboards
- no hands up
- multiple-choice quizzes
- hinge questions
- homework
- live feedback.

For us, curriculum-related expectations and assessment are intrinsically linked. Our journey with them is ongoing – there is still development needed and we know that the curriculum changes all the time – but the most valuable thing about them is that they provide a strong foundation for each of our topics. Every teacher knows what we are teaching and why we are teaching it, and we can measure the success of our implementation through our assessment methods.

Part three

The nuts and bolts of leadership

Chapter 8
Leading department meetings

This chapter covers:

- delivering department meetings that value professional development over admin
- writing an effective weekly bulletin for your English department
- a structured meeting in four parts: a) research-linked think piece; b) main body of the meeting; c) culture critique; and d) beautiful work
- a robust process of standardisation and moderation in English.

You are in a department meeting – leading one, even – and you know what everyone is thinking: *Surely, this could have been an email?* We have all been there, right?

So often, an English department meeting becomes purely administrative: notices and a reminder for key dates and deadlines. As a leader, though, it is your responsibility to make sure that your team is invigorated in department meetings – and also, most importantly, that they learn from the experience. An effective meeting will make your team stronger than prior to the meeting's beginning. If it does not do that, the chances are that it will become a date in everyone's calendar that becomes a burden more than anything else.

This chapter offers a structure and practical suggestions for what you should include in an English department meeting to get the best out of your time.

The Weekly Bulletin

Before we get to the meetings themselves, one method of ensuring that administration is managed outside of sacred meeting time is through the use of the Weekly Bulletin. This is a form of communication that tackles key dates/deadlines, notices, updates, etc.

These do not need to be communicated in face-to-face meetings with your team.

I structure my Weekly Bulletin using the following sections:

1. **Meetings and deadlines:** These might include department meetings, whole-staff meetings and data deadlines.
2. **News and updates:** Examples include details of visitors, updates to resources and the school priority focus.
3. **Key reminders:** These are always linked to routines, e.g. *Ensure that you hold the highest expectations of verbal responses in 'I say, you say' – all students should match your volume.*

The remaining sections perhaps require more detailed exemplification, so I will provide examples to support each of these.

4. Staff shout-out

I choose one member of staff each week and use lesson observation notes to capture an example of best practice to share with the team. This is a simple way in which to show how you value your staff and build a culture of teamship (see page 21).

Great use of active monitoring – you were walking around the room giving students live feedback. This is possible due to the incredible learning environment that you have created – all students were engaged, determined and taking ownership of their learning.

5. Teaching and learning

This section is always focused on an aspect of subject-specific pedagogy on which we are working collectively as a team. It is important that this is always over-communicated to staff and places value on the most important thing for your team to get right: high-quality teaching English teaching, leading to better outcomes for students.

This example links to teaching metaphor and teaching statements, discussed in Chapters 4 and 5.

I suggest two tweaks to the team's understanding and enaction of the curriculum. You could signpost these in the bulletin and delve into them more deeply in the meeting itself, or use them as a follow-up to a meeting – or both.

Tweak #1: Tenor and vehicle

We have been wrestling with our definitions of tenor and vehicle to support our explicit teaching of metaphor. I think that I have solved this by having settled on an agreed definition, and I will update the knowledge map to reflect this:

- *metaphor: any description of an object or action in a way that is not literally true*
- *tenor: the object or action being described (e.g. 'Juliet')*
- *vehicle: the language used to show that the description is not literally true ('the sun')*

Tweak #2: The flexibility of thesis statements

With thesis statements, we need to show students their flexible nature. This will be explicit in Year 10, but can be done in Key Stage 3 too.

For example, you may wish to use PLACE to front thesis statements when explicitly modelling for Romeo and Juliet.

Prior to meeting Juliet [PLACE], [COMMA] Shakespeare [NAME] conveys [VERB] love as a source of pain for Romeo [POINT] when describing it as a 'choking gall' [QUOTATION].

6. Reading reflections

Encourage your team to explore a blog, book or research paper that might spark debate and discussion around teaching and learning in the English department. You can also share what you are reading with your team and what is shaping your current thinking as department leader.

Teachers in my department frequently comment on how much they enjoy this section. It is important to note that as a leader you want to stimulate discussion within your team and pique their intellectual curiosity. My team loves sharing their thoughts on our reading reflections and how this has shaped their teaching practice.

This week, I have been musing on our oracy through the use of 'turn and talk'. This blog by Tom Sherrington outlines three principles to enable effective paired talk. These guiding principles are incredibly sound to ensure that 'turn and talk' and habits of discussion have a return on investment in terms of time used in a lesson.

https://teacherhead.com/2024/04/10/getting-pair-talk-right-its-not-that-complicated-but-its-more-than-having-a-chat-three-golden-rules

From this reading, I want to ensure that we all follow these three principles in the English department:

1. *Ensure that every student speaks and listens.*
2. *Ensure that all students can access the knowledge to think with.*
3. *Structure the question to scaffold for access and depth.*

7. Curriculum

Revisit an area of curriculum planning. This may have been the focus of a previous meeting. Again, this gives your team an insight into your thinking, planning and reflecting as a leader, and provides a clear mental model of how you want your team to think about the curriculum delivery as a whole.

Leading department meetings   **177**

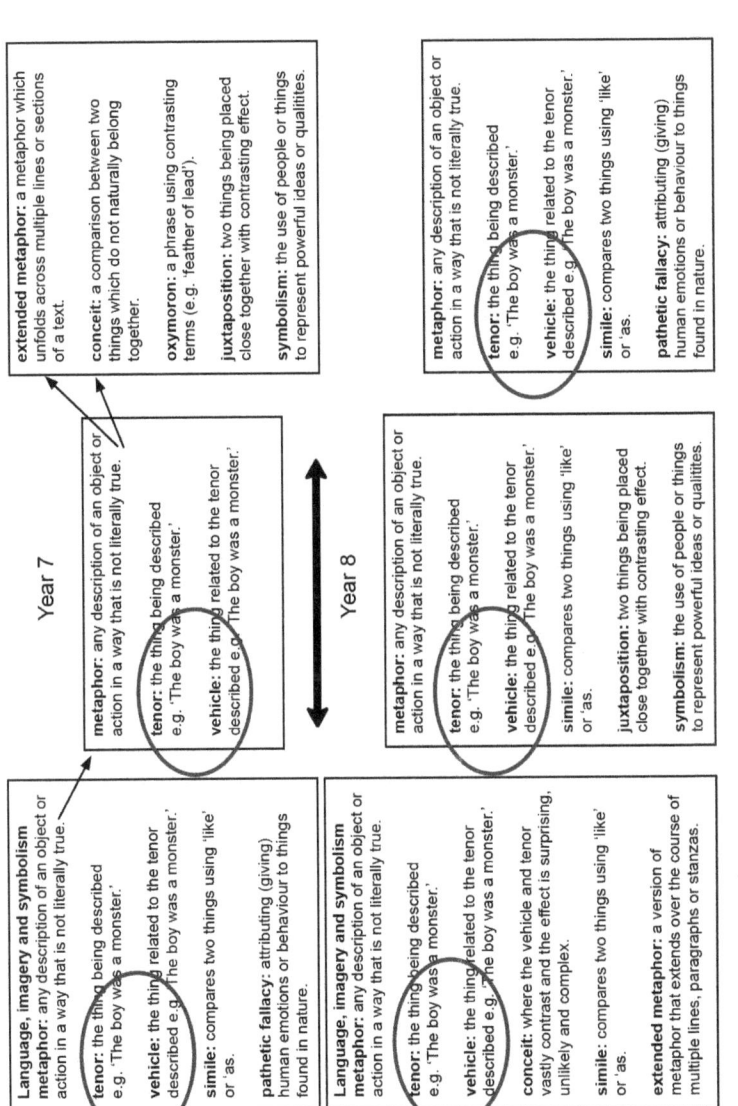

FIGURE 16: Spiral curriculum mapping

Figure 16 references the knowledge map referenced in Chapter 6.

As part of the curriculum review, I presented our spiral curriculum model, where knowledge is explicitly mapped out to be taught, and then revisited with increasing levels of difficulty. You can see this really clearly in Figure 16 when you consider how we teach metaphor...

This is not a coincidence. Remember that everything we do is intentional.

8. Assessment and data

As you read in Chapter 7, assessment in English is only worthwhile if it helps to shape the delivery of your curriculum for the better. Therefore, how you present this to staff in your bulletin will mirror the philosophy that underpins your assessment.

For example, if you are using curriculum-related expectations, this section can be used to highlight areas for development arising from your curriculum model:

A reminder that students are struggling to include an effective POINT in their thesis statements. We need to model how this should help to develop a line of argument in a paragraph.

Let's look at a typical response from the recent Year 7 enquiry question: How does Shakespeare portray Juliet's agency throughout the play?

Shakespeare [NAME] portrays [VERB] Juliet's agency [NOT A POINT] during Paris's attempts to gain Capulet's approval of their marriage [PLACE], [COMMA] with 'my will to her consent is but a part'. [QUOTATION]

In this example, we need to make clear to students that their POINT is a moment of interpretation of Juliet's agency – does she possess agency? Is agency lacking?

Therefore, the POINT should be something like: Juliet is having some element of agency because Capulet is implying in the QUOTATION that she has an element of choice in marriage to Paris.

Setting up a space for discussion with your team about common hurdles in the curriculum is more powerful to report back to your team than raw assessment scores, grades, indications of students being below target, etc. This form of data helps to inform teaching and learning and addresses gaps forming in the curriculum to ensure that all teachers in the English department are rowing together towards the same goal.

The structure of a department meeting

As you may have guessed by this point, I like consistency, routines and the predictability that arises from those. Therefore, I also advise an element of consistency in the structure of English department meetings.

I structure meetings into four parts:

- research-linked think piece
- main body of the meeting
- culture critique
- beautiful work.

Research-linked think piece

I often begin an English department meeting with a research-linked think piece. It establishes a culture where thought, debate and reflection are the norm and ensures that meeting time is not just reserved for administrative purposes.

This really gives your team the opportunity to think intellectually and reflect on their teaching. It is incredibly important for their professional development, and department meetings are a great place in which to facilitate group thinking and development.

Aim to choose a think piece that has a practical component to it. It must be used to inform teaching and learning and act as a springboard to improve the classroom practice of teachers. Consider what you want the think piece to do? You want your think piece to open up different approaches to the curriculum content, to spark new insights and to keep your department motivated.

For example, I wanted to introduce a department approach towards teaching grammar to improve students' own sense of authorial intent as writers and to increase their skill and confidence in analysing text. I drew from the work of the 'grammar as choice' pedagogy by Debra Myhill (2020) and the University of Exeter as a research-linked think piece.

I briefly outlined the underpinning principles of the Exeter pedagogy, namely that the creative grammar-writing relationship can be fostered through:

- explicitly teaching grammatical points **relevant to learning about writing**
- developing young writers' knowledge about language and **how language choices shape meaning** in the texts that they read
- developing young writers' understanding of the **language choices that they can make** in their own writing.

I supplemented this with the pedagogical framework that was developed by Myhill and her team, summated as LEAD principles, shown in Table 18 overleaf.

Doing this articulated my thinking process to the team as a leader. I wanted to clearly model that my decisions in implementing our curriculum were research-informed, but I also wanted to be really precise about where the influences in my thinking stemmed from, to mitigate any misinterpretations when it came to the team applying these principles in their classrooms.

In order to achieve this, I had to then offer a concrete example of how this research was enacted through *our* curriculum. At the time, we were teaching *The Art of Rhetoric* to Year 8, so I wanted to show the team how the LEAD principles influenced how we taught the impact of grammatical choices in Barack Obama's 2008 victory speech.

With the team, I used this as an **authentic text** to exemplify how the 'grammar as choice' pedagogy would shape our teaching of this piece of rhetoric. The **example** from the speech that I used was:

TABLE 18: Grammar as choice LEAD principles

PRINCIPLE	EXPLANATION	RATIONALE
LINKS	Make a **link** between the grammar introduced and how it works in the writing being taught	To establish a purposeful learning reason for addressing grammar and to connect grammar with meaning and rhetorical effect
EXAMPLES	Explain the grammar through showing **examples**, not lengthy explanations	To avoid writing lessons becoming mini-grammar lessons and to allow access to the structure even if the grammar concept is not fully understood
AUTHENTIC TEXTS	Use **authentic** texts as models to link writers to the broader community of writers	To integrate reading and writing and to show how 'real' writers make language choices
DISCUSSION	Build in high-quality **discussion** about grammar and its effects	To promote deep metalinguistic learning about why a particular choice works and to develop independence rather than compliance

'This election had many firsts and many stories that will be told for generations. But one that's on my mind tonight's about a woman who cast her ballot in Atlanta. She's a lot like the millions of others who stood in line to make their voice heard in this election except for one thing: Ann Nixon Cooper is 106 years old.'

I then modelled the learning sequence that might follow, to ensure that the **links between grammar and meaning** were explicit to students. I offered the following question: *How does the use of the quantifier 'many' set up how special Ann Nixon Cooper is?* As a team, we discussed the potential meaning that may be elicited from this grammatical choice.

Finally, to enable **discussion** around grammar as a choice, I would ask students to participate in a 'turn and talk' with the prompt question: *Why is Obama doing this?*

It is far more effective to put theory into practice and offer concrete examples of how the research-based approach that you have proposed can slot into your existing curriculum. This way, you are more likely to encourage others to adopt or even just try out new and varied teaching methods.

Main body of the meeting

This will vary from meeting to meeting, depending on what your priorities are at a particular stage in your department's journey. The main body is what the particular focus for that meeting is. Remember, though, that this is not an opportunity for completing administrative tasks. This needs to be training. Your team needs to leave the department meeting stronger than they entered it. This will not happen if you are reading a list of key dates, deadlines or notices from a PowerPoint slide. Again, do not let your department think that 'This could have been an email'.

What do you focus on then? Training your English department can be broken into three key areas to develop and strengthen your team:

1. subject knowledge
2. subject-specific pedagogy
3. standardisation and moderation

1. Subject knowledge

As a leader, you will need to gather information from your team and find out where the subject knowledge gaps are. This can be done with SKA (subject knowledge audit) or through your one-to-one meetings with team members. This could then inform this section of your department meetings, and other teachers who have more in-depth knowledge can then teach the group during this section as part of a collaborative process of CPD.

Knowledge within the discipline of English is highly varied and often complex. It is important to remember that not every member of your team will possess the same level of subject knowledge when you design your curriculum.

For example, if you are teaching *The Art of Rhetoric* to Year 8, it might be that not all the teachers in your department know about Aristotle's artistic proofs. They then might not confidently deliver your curriculum, where you have stated that students should know and use ethos, pathos and logos. If teachers in your team are aware of these terms, you want to identify how in-depth their knowledge is and how that might affect their teaching of a particular topic or concept.

It is your job to ensure that your staff has sufficient subject knowledge with which to deliver your knowledge-rich curriculum, accounting for all the obstacles that students might encounter. Yet this is often overlooked by leaders, or at least not prioritised highly enough.

One possible reason for this is its lack of emphasis in ITT or the Early Career Framework (ECF) (DfE, 2019). For example, it is important to acknowledge that only *one* out of the eight standards refers explicitly to subject knowledge: Teachers' Standard 3 ('demonstrate good subject and curriculum knowledge'). But subject knowledge is the foundation upon which all the other Teacher Standards are built. Students cannot make good progress (TS2) or plan and teach well-structured lessons (TS4) without the prerequisite subject knowledge.

Chapter 9 looks at how you develop subject knowledge within your team in much greater detail, to ensure that students get the best out of your curriculum – specifically, how you might use lectures, CPD videos and even 'walking talking mocks' for your staff.

2. Subject-specific pedagogy

As discussed in Chapter 6, it is important to establish subject-specific pedagogy within the culture of your department for consistency. It also helps to upskill your staff and makes them better classroom teachers. A department meeting needs to always have this as its goal if it is to be effective.

The key to success is in ensuring that what you model in this section of your meeting (for example, using tenor, vehicle and ground to teach metaphor) has relevance to what you are about to teach. Pre-empt this for your department so that they can put the training into action in a real-life classroom scenario as soon as possible.

Your job as a leader is to identify the opportunities within your curriculum mapping to drop in this training at the appropriate moment, in order to maximise its impact. For example, if you know that your department are teaching Year 7 Gothic writing and are likely to be teaching a particular text in the new few days or next week, then you need to ensure that you draw on examples that reflect or relate to the curriculum delivery.

Example scenario:

Teachers have recently taught the metaphor 'his blood ran cold' to Year 7 students during their study of *Frankenstein*. You noticed during lesson drop-ins and in a book look that students struggled to identify the tenor and therefore make meaningful comments on the ground of the metaphor. Your training, then, should have two purposes: first, to address the issues with the pedagogical approach to this metaphor, and second, to consider when next in the curriculum teachers could improve their teaching of metaphor and use this concrete example in your training.

To address the first issue, you need to explore with your team why misconceptions arose from the teaching of the metaphor 'his blood ran cold'. I encountered this exact scenario, so I can detail my team's response:

- Students too often expect to find the tenor of the metaphor within the text. Whilst this is true in some classic metaphors (e.g. 'Juliet is the sun', where Juliet is the tenor), often metaphors work in more complex ways.

- Due to this, students wrongly identified 'his blood' as the tenor. However, the subject of the metaphor exists outside of the text. It is the character's *sense of fear*.

- When teaching how metaphors work, therefore, think carefully about your sequencing. Draw students' attention to the vehicle first by asking them to consider the language that is non-literal. In this case, it is the fact that blood cannot literally run

cold. Absorbing 'blood' into your explanation pre-empts the misconception that 'blood' is the tenor.
- Think carefully about how you explain this in a written form. Use scaffolding to support students' conceptual understanding of the ground, perhaps with this sentence stem: *The author describes the character's 'blood' as running 'cold' in order to convey…*

By unpacking with your team what went wrong this time, they are likely to improve their teaching next time. Signpost to your department an opportunity to improve their practice in the near future. I asked the team to consider how they would teach metaphor in this passage from chapter one of Daphne du Maurier's *Rebecca* (which they would soon be teaching):

> 'The drive was a ribbon now, a thread of its former self, with gravel surface gone, and choked with grass and moss. The trees had thrown out low branches, making an impediment to progress; the gnarled roots looked like skeleton claws.'

I asked the team to work in pairs to learn sequence using the explicit teaching of metaphor (tenor, vehicle and ground) with the following examples:

- The metaphor of a 'thread' highlights a sense of fragility.
- The simile 'like skeleton claws' reinforces images of death and decay.
- The personification of 'the drive' suggests that it is being murdered ('choked').

During our feedback, staff then had actionable teaching strategies that they could adopt in their own classroom and make their own, in order to improve their subject-specific pedagogy. The collaborative element of this also built up a sense of teamship, whilst strengthening their shared understanding of how the curriculum design shaped their pedagogy – much better than a death-by-PowerPoint presentation of notices in my view.

3. Standardisation and moderation

As covered earlier, assessment in English is a thorny issue. I mentioned in Chapter 7 that it is incredibly difficult to standardise and moderate marking in a subject that has multiple correct answers. You might argue, therefore, that standardisation and moderation at an individual department level is futile, given the volatility of our exam system, but it is still vital that *your* team have a consistent understanding of how mark schemes work, what a Level 4 in Literature Paper 2 looks like, etc. Otherwise, it makes your job as a curriculum leader impossible to identify trends or patterns of underperformance, and means that any intervention you are likely to apply might not be as effective.

Within these terms, standardisation is an important function of your role. You have oversight of the internal performance data of your department, so it needs to work at some level for you and your context at the very least.

The purpose of standardisation within your department is quite simple. It is to establish a common standard of marking *within your department*. Don't get bogged down debating the flaws of external exam-based systems. Your central aim is for everyone in your department to agree that Johnny's *A Christmas Carol* essay should probably be awarded 24/30.

The process that you adopt to achieve this may vary from mine, but the important thing to note is that you do need a robust process to ensure consistency across your team. My preferred approach to standardising an assessment is this:

1. Before any member of the department looks at any student answer, meet with your team to mark five scripts collaboratively.

2. These scripts should be chosen and vetted by you (i.e. marked by you first). Ideally, they should cover the breadth of a mark scheme. For example, if marking an AQA Literature Paper 1 question on *A Christmas Carol*, you want scripts that are likely to be awarded Level 2, Level 3, Level 4, Level 5 and Level 6 of the mark scheme. (I tend not to bother with Level 1, as responses that are often marked as 'simple' or 'limited' tend to be self-evident.)

3. Photocopy enough scripts at each level for all members of your department. Provide copies of the mark scheme too. Create a booklet for this and (really important, I think) sequence the scripts in a random order, rather than ascending or descending order. This adds a desirable difficulty to the process and removes any gaming of the system.
4. Individual teachers are then given time to mark each script. You may advise them to annotate their scripts, but I do not feel that that is wholly necessary. The mark awarded is the most important thing at this stage.
5. Lead the team through each script and ask them to present their mark and their justification (e.g. 'This is clearly Level 2, as there is only some awareness of authorial methods, rather than a clear understanding).
6. After each script has been discussed, reveal what mark *you* gave it. Check for anomalies and be ready to work more closely with members of your team who fall out of tolerance, i.e. +/-3 marks to the mark that you awarded.
7. Those who successfully complete moderation can now continue marking their own scripts. Those who are unsuccessful need to attend further training with you until they continue marking.

With the final step, you might find yourself in a difficult conversation with someone. They might not agree with you. You must hold the line. Act like you are the senior examiner in this context; otherwise, the lack of consistency will mean that any dataset you accrue for your department's marking will disallow you from taking any actions with it, as you will not be able to trust it.

Moderation follows the following system, whilst the teachers in your department mark their individual scripts. Again, make this a robust process that you stick to no matter what – if not this process, then an equally well-thought-out one.

1. Teachers mark **three** scripts and then STOP. At this point, you review the scripts and decide whether the staff member can

continue marking or needs further training. Again, use the +/-3-mark tolerance.

2. Teachers mark **50 per cent** of their scripts and then STOP. At this point, you review a sample of the scripts (three to five) and decide whether the teacher can continue marking or needs further training. Again, use the +/-3-mark tolerance.

3. Teachers mark **100 per cent** of their scripts and then STOP. At this point, you review a further sample of the scripts (three to five) and decide whether the teacher can continue marking or needs further training. Again, use the +/-3-mark tolerance.

I appreciate that this feels like a lot of work for you as an individual, but it is vital and might even inform future curriculum mapping, as you collectively unveil which areas need an alternative teaching approach or further study. To lighten the load, you could also use your deputy (if you have one) or delegate the moderation review process to trained examiners in your department and quality-assure their work. However you manage to make it work, know that it pays dividends when you are challenged by your SLT about data.

Culture critique

This is an opportunity in your department meetings to conduct a health-check on your department's culture. The best way in which to do this is to centre this on the habits and routines that you establish, as discussed in Chapter 2.

For example, if you have stated that each teacher in your department should use 'three, two, one, whiteboards', this is a great time at which to evaluate its effectiveness. During your lesson drop-ins, you will have noticed great practice and areas for development. This can be captured and used to upskill staff in this section of your meeting.

My advice is to always begin by identifying good practice and use this as a lever for improving pedagogy, rather than point out examples of poorer practice. For instance, you might tell your team about specific examples where mini-whiteboards were used very effectively:

In Ms A's lesson, she used MWBs to 'check for understanding' when teaching the metaphor 'his blood ran cold'. She expertly identified the few students who understood that the vehicle included both 'blood' and the notion of this running 'cold'. But it also meant that she recognised that most students did not understand the vehicle choice fully and she was therefore able to reteach to better secure students' understanding.

From here, you can ask staff to reflect on their lessons tomorrow. Are there opportunities to use 'three, two, one, whiteboards' to achieve a similar goal to Ms A? This can lead to discussion and collaborative planning and, crucially, it might enhance what a teacher does in the classroom immediately in a concrete or tangible way.

Beautiful work

In *An Ethic of Excellence* (2003), Ron Berger claims that 'if you're going to do something, I believe, you should do it well. You should sweat over it and make sure it's strong and accurate and beautiful and you should be proud of it.' (Berger, 2003, p. 8). I could not agree more.

Much of what I have covered in the book so far is sweating every detail to ensure that what you and your team do each day results in *beautiful work*.

Therefore, it makes sense to end your department meeting on a note of celebration. You want to motivate and inspire your team, so offer them an example of what you have witnessed that is truly beautiful. This will depend on you and your context, of course, but I think that it should be linked to teaching and learning, rather than acts of kindness.

For example, I ended a department meeting once with what a student said about a teacher during a lesson spotlight. It was joyful for us all to indulge a little bit in our success. It is also a great metric of your department's culture of teamship when you see how happy other members of the team are about the beautiful work of an individual (side before self, remember?).

> *Sir has helped me to achieve things this year that I did not know were possible. I never understood about nouns and adjectives really in*

primary school and now I get it. I get that adjectives modify nouns to make a clear picture in my reader's head. I get that the choice I make affects how readers understand my characters. I just get it.

Now that is beautiful work.

Speaking of beautiful work, this chapter ends with another fantastic case study from Elaine McNally and her approach to leading English department meetings. Elaine is an experienced English teacher, former head of department and now assistant headteacher, with a responsibility for teaching and learning. Over the course of many years, she has taught a wide range of students in varied settings. As a head of department, she managed a large department, leading significant improvements in departmental efficiency to build a culture of continuous development. Through her writing and speaking, she contributes to the development of subject-specific knowledge and shares educational resources. She is also the author of a study guide with The Quotation Bank.

Case study: Leading department meetings

Elaine McNally

Department meetings are critical for professional development, collaboration and the strengthening of subject knowledge. However, they can become dominated by too much administration. Admin is important: without solid systems in place for assessment, curriculum planning and behaviour management, staff are unlikely to feel secure. But once admin systems are sorted and running smoothly behind the scenes, then meetings can be used profitably to develop subject knowledge and pedagogy – which, if I'm honest, is the bit that I find most motivating and interesting!

To build subject knowledge and refine subject-specific teaching practices, sometimes meetings need to shift from a top-down structure to a collaborative environment where everyone can contribute ideas, share knowledge and try out new strategies. Get this culture right and the role of a department leader can then be more about coordinating than directing. It's less about telling and more about encouraging, sharing and experimenting together.

To foster an environment where subject knowledge can grow, I've used all of the following practical strategies at one time or another:

- Professional resources like Litdrive and Massolit are absolute goldmines, but there's so much out there – blogs, books, journal articles, NATE, EMC – that connect to the latest research and teaching ideas. Share these regularly in meetings or newsletters, to excite your team about subject knowledge and to keep an academic conversation going.
- My favourite professional development is just sitting down as a team, working through a poem or text and making notes together. This helps us to see things from different perspectives, spot potential student misconceptions, plan questions and explanations, and agree on how we want to teach certain things.
- Use the meeting time to watch a video from the exam board or one that offers an approach to teaching an aspect of the language GCSE. I really like doing this, as it generates lots of discussion.
- Encourage your team to lead sessions on their areas of expertise. It's a great way in which to foster a culture where we all learn from each other; no one needs to be the expert on everything.

Example: How we embedded a sentence-level writing curriculum

In the summer of 2022, our English department embarked on a project to embed a sentence-level writing curriculum, aimed at developing students' writing skills. This was based on the principles of deliberate practice and shared expertise.

We started by auditing staff knowledge through a questionnaire, using department meetings to reflect on our writing practices. Even though writing is something that we do in every lesson, the audit exposed gaps in how we collectively approached teaching it. The questionnaire sparked important discussions: What were we truly trying to achieve in our writing lessons? What changes did we want to see in both our students and our teaching? Crucially, I knew that, in doing this audit, I was acknowledging my own weaknesses as well as those of the department. If I expected honest responses, I had to step away from the idea that, as head of department, I knew best. Improvement isn't about top-down direction; it's about creating a safe environment, where everyone feels comfortable acknowledging strengths and weaknesses. For genuine progress, staff need to trust that their input is valued and that we're working as a team.

What became clear was that we needed a more focused approach. So, we concentrated on teaching a core set of sentence stems – phrases with the potential to elevate student responses. This was not about teaching formulaic writing, but about helping students to hold thought, negotiate complex ideas and improve their expression.

Our next step involved collaborative planning in our department meetings. Each session was tightly focused on specific content, beginning with the exploration of a single sentence stem or using subordination with a limited range of conjunctions. We made sure to get granular: what the explanation was, how the grammar works and how we planned to teach it. We even talked through potential misconceptions that might trip students up, and wrote sentence examples to see where they might struggle.

Each session built on the last. We'd recap the previous work, using quick quizzes or examples (and non-examples) from our own lessons to keep the momentum going. These discussions were highly motivating and energising. Our meetings became opportunities for professional learning, where every teacher could contribute their expertise and experiences. That's when we really started refining our teaching approach as a team. I created space for this subject-specific training by keeping admin to a minimum, sharing as much as I could through emails and a department newsletter, but mostly by being really strict with how I allocated time. I wanted to use our time for this; it was important, so I made it work.

Crucially, we used our meeting time to collaborate on scripting explanations and creating resources to ensure consistency in content delivery. Codifying key aspects of the subject is powerful because it fosters professional equity; everyone brings different strengths but, by working together, we ensure that all students receive the same high-quality teaching. This approach wasn't about imposing rigid routines; it was about creating a shared language and understanding in order to encourage adaptive expertise. One of the best things that came out of this whole process was the way in which it strengthened our department culture. By identifying and naming specific practices, we made it so much easier to discuss, refine and collaborate.

I firmly believe that meetings should have a clear goal. At their core, department meetings should provide clarity and direction, so that everyone is clear on what we're doing, why we're doing it and how we can do it better. Every time we attend a department meeting, we should know what we're there to achieve. A productive meeting might focus on a specific strategy, creating actionable steps: *Here are three sentence structures that we'll be using with Year 10. By the end of this meeting, we'll all know how to teach students to write thesis statements using these structures.* That's something that you can walk out of the meeting and actually do in your classroom the next day.

This whole approach to department meetings – keeping the admin to a minimum, putting subject knowledge front and centre and creating a culture of collaboration – offers a powerful model for professional development. By keeping things clear, using shared language to codify the practice that we want and focusing on deliberate practice, we've built a department that can work together to improve teaching and learning in a meaningful and sustainable way. In the case of our writing curriculum, this approach helped to improve student outcomes, strengthen teacher confidence and build a collaborative culture that continues to grow.

Chapter 9
Subject knowledge and expertise

This chapter covers:

- exploring your team's subject knowledge
- the importance of developing your team's subject knowledge
- specific strategies to develop expertise, including booklets, a lecture series, CPD videos and walking talking mocks.

Leading a team of English teachers is often leading a group of intellectual powerhouses. Subject knowledge lies at the heart of any effective English teacher whom you will lead. You cannot teach English expertly through generic approaches to teaching and learning; staff need to be experts in the area of the curriculum that they are delivering.

However, I don't believe that this necessarily means that a degree in English is a prerequisite to being an expert English teacher. I have worked with some brilliant English teachers who do not hold a degree in English. Conversely, I have worked with English degree holders who inevitably had gaps in their knowledge of certain curriculum areas but were true experts in their classroom.

The complexity of this area also arises when you consider the disconnect between what you might have studied in your English degree and the curriculum that you deliver at a secondary school. For example, in my undergraduate degree, I studied two modules that might support my subject knowledge of texts that I have taught in secondary school:

- Victorian literature (*A Christmas Carol*, *The Strange Case of Dr Jekyll and Mr Hyde*, *Oliver Twist*)
- introduction to Renaissance literature (*A Midsummer Night's Dream, Romeo and Juliet, Macbeth, Much Ado about Nothing, King Lear*).

In essence, mostly Shakespeare and Dickens. Saying that, none of the texts above appeared on any reading list for these modules.

Modules that I studied that have no direct impact on the subject knowledge required to teach most curricula in secondary English included:

- twentieth-century American literature
- late medieval literature
- women's writing 1680–1830
- Irish literature
- marvels, monsters and miracles in Anglo-Saxon England.

With a carefully designed curriculum, teachers in your department need a high level of expertise in terms of subject knowledge of *that* curriculum.

They must also exude a passion for the curriculum to students in their classroom. This is made clear in the Teaching Standards, where Teaching Standard 3 states that teachers must 'have a secure knowledge of the relevant subject(s) and curriculum areas, [and] foster and maintain pupils' interest in the subject' (DfE, 2021b, p. 11).

Now for a moment of honesty. I do not love everything in the curricula that I have delivered – even the curricula that I designed myself from scratch.

Yet I defy you to ask any of my students – current or previous – whether at any point during lessons I appeared disinterested in the subject area that I was teaching. In fact, some of the curriculum areas I have taught that I disliked the most led to my most passionate teaching of them. I think that this is important. We cannot expect students to remain engaged in English lessons if the expert at the front of the room is disinterested. Sometimes, you need to remind yourself and your team that there is a performative element to teaching. You sometimes need to fake it to make it.

Your job as the leader of an English department, therefore, is to enable your team to meet Teacher Standard 3, regardless of their individual passions, stage of their career or subject knowledge.

I outline numerous strategies that will aid you in supporting your team to develop their subject knowledge and expertly deliver your curriculum. These include:

- booklets
- a lecture series
- CPD videos
- walking talking mocks (for staff).

But before, we get into these strategies, I want to introduce a case study from Miriam Hussain, who argues passionately about the priority of a leader in securing subject knowledge for all members of an English department. Miriam Hussain is an assistant principal for United Learning. She is a teacher of English and author of *Ready to Teach: An Inspector Calls*. Much of what Miriam covers through her case study mirrors my own suggestions, so it useful to read these side by side.

Case study: Securing subject knowledge

Miriam Hussain

I have worked in a number of English departments in my career in education and what I have found to be pivotal is that it is critical for teachers to have a secure understanding of a curriculum prior to teaching the text to students. If teachers do not have a strong subject knowledge of the topic at hand, they simply will not be able to teach it well. For this case study, I have split the chapter into four components: collaborative planning sessions, resource packs, CPD and centralised resources.

1. Collaborative planning sessions

Planning sessions should be organised regularly to discuss the text in detail. I have done these weekly within a school with a large ITT cohort and fortnightly for more experienced staff. It is all dependent on the needs of the department. These sessions are led by various individuals within the department. It is important to note that not every CPD session can be led by the head of department, so being able to rely on your team is important. One person should not lead all initiatives; otherwise, you are relying on one individual for everything, which creates a very high-pressure environment. It is also the main reason why transformational leadership fails as a result (Rees, 2019). What I have found to be useful is to make sure that there is a model and template in place to ensure that the meetings run well. Other teachers then have the format of how to deliver a meeting. This not only empowers others but also gives them valuable experience in leading teams. It is also a crucial component of their development to be able to organise and lead a planning session. This is why it is significant to have department or faculty working parties. The time itself gives an opportunity to discuss key themes, character development, understanding of the text and any historical context of note. It will also give the chance to answer questions that students will be expected to answer in lessons – this is an extremely useful task, as it really assesses a teacher's knowledge and highlights any knowledge gaps that they may have within their own understanding. Furthermore, during these meetings, teachers can be taught to and explore how they would teach the more complex topics and share best practice. Meetings in this manner foster a unified approach to teaching the text and help to codify teaching methods across the department.

2. Developing comprehensive resource packs

Creating comprehensive resource packs can serve as a valuable reference for teachers. Having established working parties within your department, it allows the creation of these booklets to be allocated to each working party within a year group. The head of department demonstrating the template for how they are to be created is useful, as the team will then have a consistent template to which to refer. These packs can include (but feel free to adapt) detailed chapter summaries, character analyses and their development, thematic explorations and any relevant contextual information. Providing teachers with these materials ensures that everyone has access to the same foundational knowledge, which can be useful for any staff member for teaching new content.

3. CPD

I mentioned collaborative planning sessions earlier in this case study, but I also wanted to touch on CPD. This CPD session may focus on specific strategies of the text or elements of knowledge that make it more detailed than the planning sessions. Before delivering any form of CPD, it needs to be calendared in and communicated. Looking over the school calendar as a whole and planning out when and where CPD takes place is crucial. This is something that requires careful consideration, thinking about whole-school deadlines and pinch points within the year – for example, data drops, marking following exams and parents' evenings. You want to be able to think about your team's wellbeing (Howard, 2020) and what their week looks and feels like as much as the pieces of knowledge that you want them to take away.

Any thriving department will need an overview of what is being taught and when. I have found weekly bulletins to be extremely useful in communicating upcoming events and deadlines. This ensures that meetings taking place focus on the conceptual and on developing your team's subject knowledge, and it enables emails to be the focus of procedural knowledge and deadlines. By sharing deadlines and calendared events in this way, it allows your department to be aware and plan for upcoming dates, whilst also setting any work that can be done prior to the meeting. This is useful for your teams, as it makes them aware of what needs to be done in advance but also of what each meeting will do. It supports the teams in preparing for the meetings and content ahead. By structuring communication and the CPD schedule in this way, it enables deadlines to be procedural and CPD be conceptional. You want to avoid people feeling like meetings 'could have been an email'. Joe Kirby's blog (2023) on upstream strategies is extremely useful with regard to this. He states that 'The more upstream you solve the problems, the less inconsistency you end up with at the end' – which is exactly what this work does. We want to be reactive with our teams and ensure preventative thinking.

CPD sessions can focus on in-depth analysis and insights into the text. I have found the John Catt *Ready to Teach* series extremely helpful here, as the books contain not only detailed resources but also detailed knowledge of the text. When teaching *Macbeth* to Key Stage 4, Pryke and Stanisforth (2020) write in intricate detail of the meaning of quotations, contextual knowledge and character knowledge. The books have really supported teacher knowledge, which is an example of how to use educational books within CPD sessions to strengthen teacher knowledge of a text. A way of maximising this knowledge and time is sending out the resource or pre-reading prior to the session, which maximises the CPD time allocated.

4. Centralised resources

The goal of CPD is for teachers to be better equipped to teach. The CPD and resource booklets support teachers' knowledge and allow them to have a secure understanding of the text. The collaborative sessions allow teachers the time to plan the resources. A way in which to give teachers feedback and to support workload (Howard, 2020) is for resources to be uploaded into a centralised area; this not only provides an opportunity for the lead teachers within the faculty to give feedback, but it also enables teachers to look at each other's work.

Booklets

I am a huge advocate for booklets as an effective vehicle for delivering an English curriculum.

Booklets can support teachers with subject content knowledge. But what exactly do we mean by this?

Subject knowledge (or subject content knowledge) sits between a university-level understanding of a subject and the student encountering the curriculum for the first time in our classrooms. It is the understanding of the concepts, principles, facts and structure of any given subject (Shulman, 1986).

For teachers of English, depending on our prior educational experiences (as students and as teachers), we will have differing subsets of knowledge with which we feel confident. Considering again my university-level education and subsets of English knowledge within that, I rarely used that specific knowledge in reality. Yet I probably do use the knowledge that sits behind it (narratology, contextual influences, language, imagery and symbolism, for example). No teacher in your department (whether they are a subject specialist or not) needs to have the knowledge of a subject expert, but they *will* need to be well versed in the subset of knowledge that relates to your curriculum.

A well-designed booklet – much like an excellent text book – can guide the teachers in your department to the knowledge that they need most in order to effectively deliver your curriculum and not be left to flounder in the vast ocean of knowledge in a particular subject domain.

This is important when the subject domain has a wide array of knowledge that you could impart to students. Teachers who feel less confident in this area may struggle with where to start, and might end up over-compensating and imparting unnecessary knowledge to students, distracting to your curriculum aims.

I have seen this happen most frequently in teaching Gothic literature, a popular subject domain in many Key Stage 3 English curricula. When I speak with teachers about their knowledge of the Gothic genre, I am always amazed by a lack of confidence in their subject knowledge of it – or, worse still, misconceptions about what Gothic literature covers; some confuse it with the genre of horror.

My university experience meant that I was a novice in the genre when I first taught Gothic literature in my NQT year, and I taught it rather badly – not because I was a bad teacher, but because my subject knowledge was poor, and so my lesson planning baked in misconceptions right from the beginning. In truth, I could not really define what Gothic literature was to students, so they never quite got it and ended up writing horror stories at the end of the unit, instead of Gothic tales…

This was evident in my opening lesson, where I asked students to give examples of Gothic stories with which they were familiar, without actually defining it (do not judge too harshly – it was 2010!). Blank stares. A muddled explanation from me about scary or spooky elements. Before I knew it, I had a bullet-point list of horror films (think *The Amityville Horror*, *Drag Me to Hell*, *Paranormal Activity*…) on my whiteboard under the title 'Gothic tales'.

To clarify (and perhaps in its simplest terms), Gothic literature comprises the following core elements:

- dark and picturesque scenery
- a narrative often akin to melodrama
- supernatural elements to evoke an atmosphere of mystery, fear and dread.

Of course, the horror films that students mentioned may have elements of the Gothic, but they were horror stories through and through – which is why students ended up producing gory, violent narratives in their end-of-unit assessment on Gothic tales. It therefore did not achieve the curriculum's aim.

This had a profound impact on me and has shaped a lot of what came later in my career to ensure that members of my department did not make the mistakes that I did.

You might already remember the knowledge map in Chapter 5 or the Golden Thread of genre distilling this into the following key terms, to support our staff and students' understanding of the core elements of the genre:

- **dark and atmospheric settings:** often created by spooky settings, such as dark forests or abandoned mansions
- **the supernatural:** things that some people believe are real, but which are not part of nature and/or are inexplicable by the scientific laws of nature
- **atmospheric dread:** a feeling of fear and foreboding.

This was to ensure a laser-sharp focus on how we defined and identified elements of the Gothic genre as a team and to ensure that no one in the department drifted into a different genre like I did many years ago.

Our booklet for this topic repeated the terms again and again and applied them to a range of Gothic texts to ensure that students were crystal clear about what Gothic is and what it is not.

To reinforce this, we added a section to the booklet that examined the differences between Gothic and horror. I wanted to pre-empt any misconceptions that might arise from staff or students, to ensure that their writing was firmly in the Gothic genre and not the horror genre.

Staff were provided with the necessary background context about the Gothic genre in relation to literature and its differences to horror, and our booklet included this for students:

> *A lot of Gothic work is about building a sense of dread, terror and suspense in the audience. This may be followed by some horrific reveal, or it may not, but atmospheric dread is key.*
>
> *It is thus important to note the difference between terror (evoked in Gothic literature) and horror. Terror is more about dread – anticipation founded in apprehension and fear (e.g. a babysitter walking around a big, empty, dark house, alone at night) – whereas horror is an innate reaction to seeing or reading something truly shocking, gory or disturbing (the killer jumps out and physically harms someone).*

Providing a booklet means that you do not have teachers scrambling around to work it out for themselves. It supports their subject knowledge and gives them the opportunity to employ a high level of subject expertise when teaching their students. It is important that all members of the department use the same resource to ensure that there is a shared understanding, and that each member of your department uses the same analogies to explain new concepts to students.

Lecture series

There is a high probability that members of your department *do* possess the knowledge of a subject expert that aligns to specific areas of your curriculum. This can – and should – be exploited to your and your team's advantage to boost subject expertise. Some of the best CPD that I have ever received has come from consummate experts within my department.

Sometimes there is nothing better than English teachers just geeking out about the subject that they teach. Presenting a space where they can do that empowers all parties – those who deliver a lecture and those who listen.

Prior to teaching a new unit of work within your curriculum, conduct a subject knowledge audit to better understand the knowledge that each member of your department has and how best to share it.

This can be a simple series of questions to get a sense of where the strengths and areas for development exist in your team.

1. On a scale of 1 to 10, how confident do you feel about your subject content knowledge prior to teaching X?
2. Ahead of teaching, in what areas of X would you like further training to support your teaching?
3. If this is an area in which you feel very confident in terms of subject content knowledge, what would be the title of your lecture to support others' CPD?

You might have other methods with which to achieve the same outcome, but the point is that you want to identify who in your team can be the resident expert on a subject domain, and use them as a lever to improve the subject expertise of others within your team.

It might be helpful for you to imagine an area within your curriculum where you feel that your subject content knowledge is a 9 or a 10 out of 10 and consider what your lecture title would be.

For me, it would be the following at each different key stage:

- Key Stage 3: *Romeo and Juliet* (Juliet and the role of female agency within the play)
- Key Stage 4: *A Christmas Carol* (a story that extols Christian values)
- Key Stage 5: *The Handmaid's Tale* (the complicity of women in Gilead's cruel patriarchy).

The lectures do not need to be long – I advise no more than 15 minutes – but they provide a wonderful opportunity for your team to use their intellectual prowess and support each other with CPD.

It is also important (as I have stated repeatedly throughout the book) that you do this first. You must lead by example and act as the mental model for your team. The lectures need to be high-quality and engaging in order for your team to benefit from them.

This may sound idealistic, or you and your department may feel time-poor. You might even question whether anyone in your team would volunteer to do a lecture.

There are always reasons *not* to do something. However, this is another mechanism for building a culture in your department. If you want to have a team of passionate subject experts, you have to cultivate that. And yes, sometimes that means pushing people outside of their comfort zone.

When I first introduced a lecture series in a previous school, these were the reasons why some members of the team felt that they could not offer the department a lecture:

- I don't know as much as X or Y, so I wouldn't be any good.
- I do not like presenting to adults. Kids are fine, but adults are scary.
- No one would care about what I would have to say about that topic.

You might also ruminate on what members of your team might say if you were to implement this method of CPD in your department.

However, you need to be brave and you need to be bold sometimes as a leader.

Should any of those concerns stop you from conducting lectures? No. In extreme circumstances, you might find yourself delivering more of the lectures to begin with. That might be necessary. If subject knowledge is poor, you are closing gaps for your team. That is your job, but over time I believe that members of your department will want to be the other voice in the room or hear from other speakers in the room.

CPD videos

This is a slightly safer option if the lecture series feels like a step too far, but it does carry the same aim: using high-quality resources to enhance the subject content knowledge of members of your team.

One thing to bear in mind is that members of your department might not be like you when it comes to the motivation to upskill their subject knowledge. By virtue of purchasing this book, you are likely to have already invested in developing your subject expertise. You might be the kind of teacher who attends conferences in your spare time, reads extensively about and around the subject of English, uses social media to keep abreast of education developments and therefore probably accesses CPD videos independently already.

This is not a given for all teachers that you lead. Therefore, your team needs your leadership to steer them towards accessing CPD videos that you feel that your department could benefit from watching.

You have two options here: create in-house videos and share them across your team as a vehicle for subject knowledge CPD, or look for online resources. There is a wealth of high-quality teaching material in the English teaching community online.

There are two online resources that I feel are incredibly useful from which to draw as you develop your team's subject expertise:

- Litdrive: a registered charity and the only English subject association that is developed and maintained by English teachers for English teachers.

- Massolit: offers over 10,000 short video lectures across 16 subjects, presented by subject experts from leading universities.

How you choose to use resources with your team is up to you.

I advise using the main body of a department meeting to watch a Litdrive online CPD video or a Massolit lecture together as a team. Doing this collaboratively (at least initially) might yield better results than expecting busy teachers to do this independently in their spare time.

To make this more of a training/development exercise, I think that you need to support staff to make the most of this CPD offer. There are multiple ways in which to do this, as outlined below:

- Explain to your team that after watching the video/lecture, you will discuss the following questions:
  a) Tell me one thing that interested you the most from the video/lecture.
  b) Tell me one thing that you disagreed with from the video/lecture.
  c) Tell me one thing that you could steal from the video/lecture to enhance your teaching of the topic.
- Prepare questions (a worksheet even) in advance, based on the video, that teachers can answer as they watch (or following watching) to discuss as a department. For example:

  Why does Professor John Bowen suggest that the Ghost of Christmas Past is a 'harsh therapist' for Scrooge?

  How does Stephen Siddall's assertion that 'the human soul is the battleground for the conflict between good and evil' apply to Macbeth's characterisation?
- Create a quiz (Massolit have these for many of the videos) that you answer collaboratively as a department.

You may have other suggestions too, or you might find that less structure works for your team. No matter how you facilitate this CPD tool, it is important that it matches your mental model of teachers enhancing their subject expertise. It should be an intellectual pursuit. As a profession, we should always strive to strengthen our subject content knowledge in the curriculum areas that we charge others to teach.

Walking talking mocks (for staff)

Whether we like it or not, our role is not just to impart knowledge in English for the love of the discipline. We need to ensure that students are exam-ready and can use the knowledge within this high-stakes environment.

One highly effective way in which to do this is through the use of 'walking talking mocks' (WTMs).

In education discourse, WTMs are widely approved – they do exactly what they promise.

The idea behind them is that students perform the entire exam experience, including sitting in the exam hall in rows, in an ideal scenario. However, instead of working diligently in silent exam conditions for the prescribed length of a given paper, a teacher leads a class/year group through the exam paper. Imagine a live modelling of the exam paper, question by question, and offering students times in between to answer questions in exam conditions.

The aim is to break down the mystifying exam techniques that one must apply to a question paper (I am looking at you, GCSE English language!) in clear and explicit steps, for students to follow and then apply all the knowledge that they have understood from their revision of the content.

I propose that you carry out the WTM with the staff in your department, to get a real feel of the exam process for students.

So, should this be the same experience as it is with the students even with staff? Yes. It is really important that your department knows what the students experience in the exam hall. The idea is that you can then reverse-engineer this back to your pedagogical approach. It is always interesting to explore the connection between how you would answer the exam question as an expert and how you instruct students to do so.

Below are some of the key reasons why I think that this is such an effective tool:

- In order to maximise student outcomes through examinations, staff require a depth of knowledge of how the exam works in practice.
- It is incredibly helpful that staff experience what the students experience in order to best prepare them for the exam.

- This allows a shared approach to exam technique as a team, ensuring that all students have a parity of experience.

Of course, you may have staff who are in fact incredibly receptive to this CPD tool. I would suggest that the vast majority of English teachers will understand the rationale of this approach and not require any of my retorts – especially if they do not have previous teaching experience with a particular exam board or are newer to the profession.

For example, a number of years ago when we did this in our department, a colleague remarked that their natural instinct for answering a *How does the writer use language to describe X* question from GCSE English language was to use multiple pieces of textual evidence with short, embedded quotations to reinforce her ideas.

When I asked whether she was teaching the students to do that, she guiltily admitted that she was not. Instead, she said that she taught them to write three PEAL paragraphs (Point, Evidence, Analysis, Link). It did not make sense, as this approach would never allow her students to deftly embed a range of quotations within an answer. This CPD session then encouraged us as a department to move away from relying on acronyms towards teaching students how to apply literary analysis, and to consider the relationship between the approach of the expert and supporting students to write in a similar fashion. This led to much higher GCSE results in English language in the subsequent years.

I want to finish this chapter with a case study from Heather Wright, a former head of English, trust director of English and currently associate principal for a multi-academy trust (MAT) in the North of England. Heather focuses on leading CPD from the front and supporting staff in their professional development through multiple lenses.

Case study: Leading staff CPD from the front

Heather Wright

The evidence is clear: teachers' engagement in professional development is widely recognised as one of the most effective ways in which to improve their ability to remain motivated, effective and capable of adapting to changes in education. The recent focus on curriculum has been a welcome one, but schools are busy places and, too often, CPD in this area can be reductive and unfocused. Without the investment in teachers' understanding, some will just see curriculum reform as another desktop exercise, filling in arbitrary forms and grids. Sometimes, as an English leader, you have to take things into your own hands and ask yourself: what can you do to maximise and invest in curriculum design CPD for teachers?

Here are some of the methods that I have used:

- **Paired academic reading:** Splitting teachers into pairs and giving them the same short burst of academic reading leads to friendly accountability, in my experience. Teachers have a buddy with whom they can chat about their initial interpretations, before bringing them, fully fledged, to a meeting with others. Think of this as 'turn and talk', but for teachers. This extra step makes all the difference.
- **Sharing nuggets of CPD:** Many teachers do not have the time or energy to read endless volumes of academic journals or 'edubooks', even if many would like to. I tend to carefully break things down into summaries, selecting passages that I know are pertinent to our current discussions, and then we take a vote in the department as to what we want to read next.
- **Framing:** One of the most successful methods that I've used for engaging teachers with CPD is framing it clearly first. Developing a narrative to showcase your learning journey together, followed by your posed question prior to reading, helps teachers to understand what we're reading for and how it builds on what we already know. For example: *Last month, we read about students relishing work above their pay grade from Mary Myatt [2021], and we decided to read more about Laura Webb's work on teaching motifs in literature to develop students' essays [2022]. We debated how this could be scaffolded appropriately for our students with SEND [special educational needs and disabilities] and, as a result, we voted to expand on this and read Christine Counsell's work on hinterland knowledge [2018]. As we're reading,*

let's ask ourselves: How would using hinterland knowledge examples support all students' understanding of motifs?
- **Key Stage 3: The wasted years?** This document had a profound effect on me when it was released by Ofsted in 2015. Yes, it was seen by some as heavy-handed and yes, it ruffled many feathers but, to me, its unmistakable message was one that no one could deny: the standard of the Key Stage 3 curricula up and down the land just wasn't good enough, and my school's Key Stage 3 English offer was no exception.

It was the same year that I had taken my first head of English role. My stock cupboard inheritance was a familiar smorgasbord of jumbled *TES* PowerPoints, photocopied worksheets and 15,000 copies of *Holes*. In short, the curriculum didn't exist and I knew that I had to start again. The biggest problem was that my department consisted of two long-term supply teachers and a busy pastoral leader, so I was largely alone in my endeavour. I spoke with my new line manager and, ignoring her warnings, made the decision to centralise the curriculum and rewrite everything over the summer. I emerged in September, ready. Was it perfect? No. Was it even good? By contemporary standards, absolutely not. But I was thrilled with it because I had poured love into every page. I knew every decision, intention and outcome and galvanised my team to believe in the same. Over the next few years, I was fortunate enough to recruit some fantastic teachers, and together we read, researched, refined, revised and rewrote our way to an evidence-led, knowledge-rich English curriculum that we were proud of. Bliss.

Fast-forward a couple of years and I had become the director of English for a northern MAT. Part of this role involved being a specialist leader in education (SLE) and working with underperforming schools across the region. It was only when I started to meet the weary and exhausted teachers in these schools that I realised just how lucky I had been to build my department from scratch without any real resistance. The teams with whom I was working hadn't just struggled to bring their English curricula up to standard; most didn't even know that they had to. Their plans not only failed to teach the well-sequenced knowledge that students would need to succeed, but they also vastly underestimated what Key Stage 2 had already equipped students with. One scheme of learning was 12 lessons of leaflet writing, half of which were dedicated to individual research on computers. Once students had eventually copied and pasted their information into their folded paper, they spent the remaining lessons decorating them. The teachers in this department defended this scheme vehemently; it was a creative unit that kids loved, they argued – nothing was wrong with it. Somewhere along the way, professional curiosity had been lost and habit had set in.

We all know that teachers can be emotionally attached to old resources and schemes. And why wouldn't they be? They often built them from nothing, usually alone on a laptop late at night or at the weekend, whilst their families made memories without them. Why would they give them up in favour of more work? In order for the teachers and leaders to see that change was necessary, I needed them to read and learn about curriculum design, because this doesn't happen by itself. Showing leaders the difference between the good and the not so good was crucial, but how could I do it without endless time and funds for educational visits?

It was clear that I needed to support leaders to reach the conclusion themselves that their curriculum needed drastic reform. I orchestrated an activity in which we were to design a summative end-point assessment for three of the schemes of work. I set boundaries for the assessment, such as 30 per cent core knowledge and 70 per cent application, just to begin with, and then worked with leaders to see what would be assessed. Quickly, colleagues saw that not only was core knowledge across the department not defined, but it wasn't being taught either. Lessons in Key Stage 3 had lapsed into GCSE-lite training grounds, with most lessons ending in tasks such as 'analyse the language in this short extract'. Silence had started to invade the room and confidence in the original schemes was slipping away. The thematic, skills-based approach was not compatible with ensuring that students in each class were receiving an equitable offer. This led to a fruitful conversation about different types of knowledge and knowledge structures for a well-sequenced curriculum. By then, the silence had stopped and glimmers of interest and excitement now punctuated the discussion. We had started.

I quickly capitalised on this intrigue and gave leaders a curated and framed reading list to inspire them – Mary Myatt (2021) for why, Daisy Christodoulou (2014) for what and Summer Turner (2016) for how – along with time to engage with it. To enable this, I would run their next interventions and meetings on their behalf and offer them some cover, whilst they read and discussed their findings, in pairs first and then together. A fortnight later, we met again and tussled with the overarching concepts about which leaders had read. With the foundations in place, we got to work on the following areas, roughly in this order:

- We led with a Pupil Premium and SEND lens; getting it right for these students was our focus, and whenever we weren't sure, we came back to their experience.
- We visited the two largest feeder primaries to learn about the local Key Stage 2 offer.
- We explored other schools' curricula and carefully considered their decisions. These schools were incredibly kind and even offered us student voice, book looks and lesson observation activities.
- We worked backwards from our end points, meaning that we had a rich debate about the chosen substantive and disciplinary knowledge, along with specific vocabulary and the vertical concepts that we wanted to be a thread across the piece.
- We developed a prototype medium-term plan for leaders in another MAT to review, and took their comments seriously.
- Finally, we held a meeting with the rest of the teachers in the department, explaining our rationale and offering carefully summarised nuggets of training and opportunities to work with leaders on schemes of learning.

Was what we produced here good? Not bad. Was it finished? Absolutely not. The real work started after this process, of course. But I left the school knowing that those leaders were ready to tackle it.

Chapter 10
Lightening the workload for your team

This chapter covers:

- quick fixes that can lighten the workload of your team – including resourcing and setting cover work
- creating a centralised behaviour system in your English department
- centralising homework as a department
- managing the pressures and workload of marking
- understanding individual ways of working.

The final chapter is less intellectually driven and less focused on the bigger-picture aspects of English. Instead it focuses on how to make the lives of your department easier in a very practical sense. I firmly believe that one of the most important jobs that you have as a leader is to make the daily teaching lives of your team as easy as possible. They will probably thank you more for this than for designing a spiral, knowledge-rich curriculum or writing a lofty destination story…

There are innumerable micro-behaviour examples of what your team do each day to ensure that they are best prepared to deliver the curriculum, assess students' progress and maximise outcomes. I want to outline as many as I can and offer suggestions for how you as a leader can support your department, not letting the small stuff detract from the larger goals held within your department's vision. Hopefully, this gives you enough to reflect on in terms of how you can make each day a little bit easier for each member of your team.

1. organising books/booklets/folders
2. eliminating the need for displays
3. avoiding lengthy queues at the photocopier
4. using a centralised behaviour system
5. using a centralised homework system
6. avoiding having to set cover whilst ill
7. reducing marking load/managing time pressures of marking
8. understanding each individual's preferred ways of working.

1. Organising books

As a leader of an English department, it is best to have a consistent approach to how students are given access to books, booklets, folders or whatever students at your school use for their written work. An agreed method of delivering that saves time and stress. Here is my suggestion:

- Ensure that all teachers in your department organise books/booklets/folders for each class that they teach so that they are accessible at all times. For example, if you have cupboards at the back of the room, provide your team with labels and ask them to organise their shelves so that all student resources are organised by class, e.g. 7A/En1, 8B/En4, 9A/En6, etc. Make sure that everyone does the same – check that everyone has done this at the beginning of the academic year.

- Create a system of a silent exit routine (see Exit 3 from Chapter 2 as an example) at the end of *every* lesson, to allow the slick transition of gathering up books/booklets/folders from the current lesson and to allow time to distribute the next set for the next lesson. It is crucial that time is dedicated for this as part of a lesson transition.

- When the teacher collects the books/booklets/folders (or perhaps later assigns a student to do this), they are collected in the *same order* every time. For example, imagine that your classroom is organised like this:

FIGURE 17: Classroom desk arrangement

  Ask students to pass along books/booklets/folders to the end of each row into a neat pile.
- You ask your team to always collect from the front to the back – row 4, 6, 4, 6, 4, 6 – so that the resources can be distributed back to appropriate desk positions next time.
- Having followed the previous step, as you then ask students to silently pack away equipment and stand behind their desks, you can focus on distributing the next class's set of books/booklets/folders. A teacher should now only need to look at a student's name, know that they sit in that first row of 4 and drop the necessary resources *at the end of the row* for students to distribute later.

With practise over time, this gets quicker and quicker, and the routine nature of this will avoid a number of issues that often arise from the distribution of resources at the beginning of a lesson – time lost, opportunities for low-level disruption and a flustered teacher greeting their students.

Establish a mental model for your team regarding the timings of this transition. For example, I would suggest that if the first lesson of the day at your school ends at 9.30 am, your team needs to end the lesson at 9.27 am to begin the silent exit routine. These three minutes should suffice in the collection and redistribution of books/booklets/folders during this allocated time.

2. Eliminating the need for displays

No one can convince me that a display has been an attributable factor to a student's success in exams.

Eliminating displays might be outside of your control as the head of the English department. It might be a mandate from your SLT that you cannot rebuke. If so, please do ask them for the evidence that displays improve student outcomes – or, indeed, ask them to consider whether they think that displays might actually be adding to students' cognitive load and affecting their performance in the classroom. This is if you feel that you can do, of course.

What should displays be used for? My ideal display is focused on one thing: showcasing students' beautiful work. My current classroom has one wall as a display, which has designated spaces (12 in total) to put up a student's work that showcases excellence in some way. That is it. Sticky tack and a photocopied page – done. It saves so much time.

What I do not advocate for is overly artistic endeavours (a blood-dripping motif piece for *Macbeth*, a crime scene investigation for *An Inspector Calls* – you know the type) that need to be regularly maintained, changed and updated, eating into a teacher's precious time. It is here where, as the leader of an English department, you need to lead by example. Even if you are dying to release your inner artist, do not do so. It puts an unfair expectation on other members of your team. It becomes a vanity project more than anything else.

If you are going to insist on displays, then focus on practicality. I suggest that all classrooms have the same displays, which *you* curate and provide. Here's what I would include:

- exam dates for that academic year (language/literature)
- a snapshot of what is included in each exam (language/literature)
- judiciously chosen quotations from your chosen literature texts.

I probably wouldn't include much else, to be honest. As I say, keep it practical. If you are able to have these created and distributed to your team, and to give them time to do this within the working day, you are at least carefully considering the time and workload pressures of the members of your department.

You might end up in a situation where a member of your department offers to invest their own time (financial resources too, perhaps) in creating a more artistic offering. You need to say no to them. They are well meaning, but they are not thinking about your team as a whole and the pressures that this creates for them. The last thing that you need is to be in a department meeting where you explain to the team that their classroom displays need to be more like Mr X's because SLT thought that it looked really engaging. Side before self, always.

3. Avoiding lengthy queues at the photocopier

In your career, consider how much dead time has been wasted in a photocopier queue. You might spend an average of 7.4 minutes in this queue per day. That will be 37 minutes each week, approximately 3.7 hours per term and 22.2 hours per academic year. That is just you. Now think of your team's numbers inflating this further. It's a huge amount of time that is not very productive.

Sometimes photocopying is necessary. However, as a leader, you can reduce this drastically in your team with changes to the operations of running your English department.

The first – and arguably most effective – method to reduce lengthy printer queues is to use booklets for your curriculum delivery. This is far more efficient. You can have booklets photocopied centrally by your admin team or an external company in advance, and you could avoid your team ever having to use the photocopier to provide curriculum materials to students. We have a 'bookletised curriculum' in our school and I genuinely almost never have to use the photocopier – it might be a few times a term.

Secondly, you can be smarter about how photocopying is used operationally within your department. For example, if you have centralised resources in the form of PowerPoints and accompanying worksheets, you can use a 'divide and conquer' method. Essentially, you make one member of your team responsible for a year group's printing – for example, Mr A is responsible for Year 7, Ms B is responsible for Year 8, etc. Each member of staff bulk-prints the required material for each unit of work for that year group. The bulk printing can be stored in a communal area within the English department, ready to be collected as and when teachers require it. You can print these as single resources (although this requires careful labelling, e.g. Y7 Term 1, Week 1) or as an anthology (i.e. a resource booklet).

Finally, think about the quality of your printed resources and whether they actually need to be printed. Communicate with your department and work out what can be streamlined. It might be the case that some members of your department are printing lots of supplementary resources that they have independently created, and this is taking up their own time. A more consistent approach to your department's curriculum delivery will help here. As the leader of the department, you must consider very carefully where the inconsistencies lie and the impact on the workload of members of staff.

4. Using a centralised behaviour system

You might be incredibly lucky to work in a school where, in your role as head of English, you don't have to supervise detentions or deal with students being removed from English lessons due to behaviour issues. In an ideal world, all schools would have centralised systems on a whole-school level that facilitate this. However, in my experience, this is rare, and the chances are that you will have some responsibility here.

The most common school systems have a sanction escalation system similar to that outlined below. These will vary from school to school.

TABLE 19: Common sanction escalation system

Behaviour detention	Removal from lesson
Step 1: The class teacher sets and is responsible for supervising a detention at break/lunchtime	Step 1: The class teacher follows the behaviour system prior to the removal option
Step 2: If a student fails to attend the teacher's detention, the student attends a detention with the head of English after school	Step 2: The head of English removes the student from the lesson or the student is placed into the classroom of the head of English if they are teaching
Step 3: If a student fails to attend the detention for the head of English, the student attends a detention with a member of SLT	Step 3: If a student continues to misbehave, they are removed by a member of SLT
	Step 4: Either the head of English or member of SLT will arrange a meeting/detention with the class teacher to reintegrate them back into their lessons

This system is fairly robust (if applied consistently at all levels), but it adds to the workload of your team quite significantly.

Here is what I would change in order to relieve the pressure on your department:

The class teacher *never* sets a detention at break or lunchtime. If a student has disrupted the lesson, I do not want to waste any more of their time. As a leader, I can take this burden from them. I use the following consequence-based system:

- C1: verbal warning
- C2: behaviour point
- C3: detention with head of English.

I understand that this is adding to *your* workload (at least initially), but it will really support your team. I promise that the work that you put in at the beginning will pay dividends in the long term – your department will be grateful and you will get more out of them as a result of your sacrifice.

My advice would also be to make this detention supervised by you a real deterrent. For example, it should be completed after school to reflect the serious nature of disrupting a lesson, and should be accompanied by a communication with parents/carers (you might find using your admin team to send a text message home an easier method than phone calls). The detention itself should not be an easy option for the student (no heads on desks!). I would create a lesson about the importance of good behaviour and deliver it as a lesson itself – make them work hard, using the same habits and routines that you would use in a standard English lesson. This will have a greater chance of students realising that it is not worth their time messing around in your colleague's lessons.

You *will* find over time (I promise) that fewer students land in your detention. If not, there is an issue with the behaviour in your department that you need to take hold of to prevent the need for these detentions in the first place. Prevention is better than cure, and your role as a leader is to establish excellent behaviour in the classrooms in your corridor. Seek support from your SLT for this too – remember that you have support systems in place to help you as a middle leader.

5. Using a centralised homework system

Setting effective homework in an English department is one of the hardest aspects of the job from my experience. Again, you may be subject to elements of whole-school policy with regard to homework setting in English, but even within those restraints, it is important to make it work for you and the members of your team.

Avoid a situation where individual colleagues are setting their own homework, with their own deadlines, and you cannot effectively monitor and evaluate its effectiveness.

You do not want to have a lack of parity in students' experiences of homework based on who their English teacher happens to be. You do not want complaints (from students, parents or SLT) to arise based on inconsistencies (*It's not fair, Mr A never sets us homework but Ms B gives us loads*). You need to have control and oversight of how and why English homework is set in your department.

There is not a definitive solution that I can offer as to what the most effective type of homework to set is for English, but I do think that there are some guiding principles that should underpin effective homework setting:

- Both teachers and students should understand the purpose of the homework set.
- Homework set should not add to teachers' workload unnecessarily.
- There needs to be a robust system for checking whether homework is complete and at the standard expected.
- Sanctions for failure to complete homework must be consistently applied.

It is fair to say that how these principles are enacted might be different depending on whether students are at Key Stage 3, Key Stage 4 or Key Stage 5. I do think that at Key Stage 5, teachers can and should be given greater control over homework setting, so the suggestions that I offer here for a centralised system are focused on Key Stage 3 and Key Stage 4 only.

Key Stage 3

This is a very specific example that might not work in your context. But as you read about it, I want you to consider how it effectively meets my guiding principles.

At Key Stage 3, students are expected to complete the following home learning on a daily basis:

1. thirty minutes of reading per day, including their compulsory task set on Sparx Reader
2. thirty minutes of recall from the knowledge organiser, using 'look, cover, write, check' or self-quizzing.

With the first task, please note that other online-reading platforms are available to use. I just happen to use (and really like) Sparx Reader, because I can set a compulsory amount of reading per week, there are in-built comprehension questions and it is easy to monitor completion rates. Also note that students can read their own books independently of using the online platform, but the point is this: regular independent reading is going to make my students better in English.

With regard to the recall task, you might not use knowledge organisers. Again, I do and I really like them. The purpose of this is to develop effective learning/revision habits early to prepare students for the demands of GCSE. There are various ways in which you could check whether students have done this, but the easiest way is to set a ten-question quiz based on the core knowledge that you have asked students to revise and set a minimum expectation of achieving eight out of ten to determine whether students have completed it. If not, sanction accordingly, as per your department or school's policy.

Key Stage 4

This is always tricky to get right. The reality is that you want students to work independently at home to ensure the best possible GCSE outcomes, but this needs to be balanced with teacher workload, which is high in an essay-based subject like English.

My suggestion is to have two strands to setting homework at Key Stage 4: **core** (the minimum that each student must complete) and **enhance** (optional, but effective for students who choose to complete it).

Core homework

For this, I defer to online platforms that allow you to create flashcards for students to revise from based on your chosen topic. You can follow up with a quiz that students complete to test their knowledge. It is simple, but highly effective in ensuring that students embed the core knowledge from your curriculum delivery into their long-term memories.

For example, if students are studying *An Inspector Calls*, you might generate a flashcard like this that students use to revise:

- Side A: Mr Birling is a dramatic vehicle for…
- Side B: capitalist greed of factory owners in pre-war Britain.

Subsequently, after students have worked their way through all the flashcards set for a topic, they answer a quiz, where the following question will appear:

> What is Mr Birling used as a dramatic vehicle for?

As with my Key Stage 3 model of home learning recall, to create accountability you need to set a minimum score that students must achieve in order for this to be considered complete. Again, 80 per cent is an excellent and fair metric for this to know whether or not to sanction.

Enhance homework

Again, imagine that students are studying *An Inspector Calls*. You might also set optional weekly tasks to complete to supplement their revision of this literature text. An example weekly task might be (but is certainly not limited to):

1. Listen to Episode 3 of the *An Inspector Calls* podcast from BBC Bitesize.
2. Write a short paragraph explaining how Priestley uses each character as a dramatic vehicle for:
   a) society's capacity to change (Sheila)
   b) misogynistic objectification (Gerald)
   c) the abusive upper classes (Eric).

6. Avoid having to set cover

Do not panic – I am not suggesting that you as the leader of the department need to set bespoke cover each time a member of your team is absent from school.

I am also not even considering cover for long-term or planned absences. Rather, this scenario is one that you and all members of your department will have encountered at some point. You are ill – too ill, in fact, to go to work – and yet you have set an alarm incredibly early to hop onto a laptop and set cover *work*. It does seem unfair really, and if you prevent your teams from having to do this, they will be incredibly grateful.

So how can you avoid this through your operation processes as a leader? Here are a few suggestions:

Knowledge organiser work

This is only applicable if you use them, of course. The cover teacher supervises students using 'look, cover, write, check' or self-quizzing of their knowledge organiser in a teacher's absence. Your ill colleague prepares nothing and the students engage in an effective session of retrieval practice.

Centralised cover booklet

Even if you do not use booklets for your curriculum delivery, have a centrally planned booklet (created by you or a member of your team) that staff can use when ill; this can relieve a lot of pressure. My advice is to have a contents page with a tick box when a page of content is complete. This will make it easier for both your ill colleague and the cover teacher, as the instruction to students is a simple one: *Please turn to the next section of your booklet and carry on from there independently.*

The content of this booklet is up to you and what works for your curriculum. In the past, I have used different approaches, ranging from generic SPaG (spelling, punctuation and grammar) resources to support technical accuracy to critical readings of the set literature texts at GCSE with guided questions. My advice is not to spend weeks sweating over the creation of this booklet and, where you can, to use resources freely available online to reduce the workload pressure of using this system.

Guided reading

I do not advocate cover simply being 50 or 60 minutes of silent independent reading. Students will not actually read, there will be a spike in low-level disruption and it feeds the view that reading is not a joyous experience.

However, what you could do is to have a question framework that supports students' independent reading to make them more accountable for the work completed in the lesson. This can be created centrally and should be relatively simple to employ.

As you read independently, complete the following tasks. All tasks must be completed by the end of the lesson.

1. *Choose one word or phrase to describe how the protagonist is currently feeling at this point in the story. Justify your choice with reference to the text.*

2. *Choose one moment from your reading today that interested you the most. Explain clearly why it interested you as a reader.*

3. *Choose one theme or big idea from your reading that you think the author is highlighting. Explain what they are saying about this in your own words.*

7. Reduce marking load

As English teachers, marking will inevitably be a huge part of our workload. To a certain extent, this is difficult to avoid compared to a subject like maths, say. However, that does not mean that we cannot do more as leaders to reduce the pressures that our department faces when it comes to marking.

One helpful wain which to do this is through whole-class feedback (WCF). I want to reiterate the point that if, as a leader, you are expecting members of your department to write extensive written comments on every student's work, then you are not supporting your colleagues with reducing their workload.

Below is an overview of the how and why of using WCF to reduce English teachers' workload.

Whilst WCF has become more commonplace in English departments, there may be members of your team who are resistant to this.

When I introduced WCF into a department that I previously led, it enraged one member of my department after I launched it. They were adamant that, after 20 years' teaching experience, they should not have to change their marking practices. However, they did eventually come around when they realised how much it reduced their workload.

In fact, my launch was centred around my attempt to reduce everyone's workload, without losing the impact of giving students feedback on work that they produced.

The example that I share here was based on a trial that I conducted with a Year 10 group who were studying *A Christmas Carol*. Sharing the findings of the trial then allowed me to introduce this new law to the department.

The approach was relatively simple:

1. Read students' recent work with no written comments. The aim was to do so in 30 minutes, accounting for the work of 25 students.
2. Write notes about what went well and what needed to be developed – initially on a scrap piece of paper.
3. That scrap of paper eventually became Figure 18.

The main criticism levelled at me when I suggested this approach was: *But how do students act on feedback without written comments?*

My response was quite simple: *Do the students need individualised comments in order to make improvements? When you do this, do students effectively act on your feedback?*

I shared the 'models of excellence' above and made the thinking behind the students' work really explicit. In fact, the named students above actually put their work under the visualiser themselves and offered a commentary as to why they wrote what they did. This was incredibly powerful: students became experts and encouraged the others to step up too.

The next step is the most crucial part: students must be able to effectively act upon a teacher's feedback.

The students are then tasked with self-assessing their needs in the form of a comparative study against the models of excellence, and they identify their own areas of improvement. Once achieved, they have time to act on their improvements independently, as shown in Figure 19 overleaf. Note: These examples were compiled in a mixed-attainment group and cover a range of abilities.

Lightening the workload for your team

Things we did well:

✓ Excellent understanding of the narrative
✓ Considered a range of ideas on the 'impacts of greed'
✓ Used supporting evidence from the text effectively
✓ Some of us analysed Dickens' methods well
✓ Some precise contextual linking e.g. Malthusian economic theory

Basic errors:

- Never use the word 'quote' in an academic essay (word/phrase/line/simile, etc.)
- Some used random capital letters in the middle of sentences
- The possessive apostrophe e.g. Scrooge's greed, Dickens' novel
- It is the Victorian era, NOT 'Victorian times'

Areas to develop/ misconceptions:

✓ Take the opportunity to analyse METHODS used in quotations e.g. juxtaposition, metaphor etc. (see example)
✓ Do not generalise the Victorian era/ society e.g. 'were all', 'common', 'majority'
✓ When analysing 'decrease the surplus population' link to Malthus (see example)
✓ 'Ignorance and Want' examples needed to extend your analysis
✓ Link to Dickens' biographical experience e.g. father went to debtors' prison, Dickens experience of poverty/ workhouses at young age

⭐ Scrooge claims that the Victorians should 'decrease the surplus population', which **uses mathematical language to suggest how to solve the problems in society. This correlates to Thomas Malthus' economic theory which states that those in poverty must die to allow for enough resources for everyone else. This depersonalises the poor in society, which makes it easier to let them die, but this is extremely unfair.** (Olivia P)

⭐ In Stave 2, Scrooge loses his love interest, Belle, due to his avaricious nature. This is seen when Belle states, 'Another idol has displaced me...a golden one'. **Dickens uses metaphor to describe money to show Scrooge cares more about this than his fiancé, highlighting his obsession with money. The noun 'idol' shows how he truly idolises money – it is what drives him and Belle feels replaced by his love for money. This highlights Scrooge's materialistic nature.** Due to his greed, Scrooge lost the love of his life: Belle was his only chance of having a family, yet he chose a lonely life instead. (Olivia U)

⭐ Dickens also presents the impacts of greed in the novel by showing the poor trapped in the poverty cycle. In Stave three, The Ghost of Christmas Present shows Scrooge two children: 'This boy is ignorant, this girl is Want'. **These two children are used as an allegory to represent children in poverty, having to resort to crime often due to the upper classes neglecting the destitute population.** The children are described as 'yellow, meagre....wolfish'. **This triparteite list shows how the greed of others impacts how impossible living whilst poor in the Victorian era was. The adjective 'wolfish' shows they are more animal than human.** (Miles)

FIGURE 18: Whole class feedback

DIRT TASKS

Considering all you have learned in the whole class feedback session, please tick off any targets that apply to your essay:

- ✓ Analyse methods in more detail, examining language choices carefully in selected evidence from the text
- ○ Develop my understanding of Dickens' intentions, by considering the **significance of ignorance and want or Malthusian economic theory** in greater detail
- ○ Make more precise links to context - avoid genaralising Victorian society
- ○ Make links to the bipgraphical details of Dickens' life where appropriate

Choose one section of your essay to improve considering your targets above and what we discussed in today's lesson:

In the extract, Scrooge's greed has an impact of ending his engagement with Belle. This is shown with Belle's claim 'another idol has displaced me'. The idol which Belle says is 'golden' is a metaphor for money and symbolises Scrooge's greed. Idols are usually objects of worship, therefore, Scrooge clearly worships wealth, rather than his potential marriage to Belle.

Essentially, Scrooge sacrifices Belle for the pursuit of money. Scrooge here represents many wealthy Victorians whose avaricious nature meant that money was far more valuable in this society.

DIRT TASKS

Considering all you have learned in the whole class feedback session, please tick off any targets that apply to your essay:

- ○ Analyse methods in more detail, examining language choices carefully in selected evidence from the text
- ○ Develop my understanding of Dickens' intentions, by considering the significance of ignorance and want or Malthusian economic theory in greater detail
- ✓ Make more precise links to context - avoid generalising Victorian society
- ✓ Make links to the bipgraphical details of Dickens' life where appropriate

Choose one section of your essay to improve considering your targets above and what we discussed in today's lesson:

[Re-doing link of Malthusian theory.]
This links to Thomas Malthus' economic theory in which he believed there is growing pressure on resources, we must let the poor die so there are enough resources for everyone else. This is very similar to Scrooge's beliefs as her depersonalises the poor in society as he sees them unworthy of living. However, this is very extreme. Some upper class people in the Victorian era also believed in this theory, like Scrooge.

[Adding Dickens' biological experience in 4th paragraph.]
This may reflect Dickens' own life, where when he was 12, his father went to debtors prison and experienced poverty at a very young age.

FIGURE 19: Student self assessment

My assertion is that this massively saves the precious time of colleagues in your department. So what time does it really save? The first table shows the time taken for conventional marking, whilst the second table shows the difference by using WCF.

TABLE 20: Conventional marking

Task	Time per student	Total time spent
Marking with written comments	5 minutes per student	125 minutes (2h 5m)
Planning a feedback (DIRT) lesson		30 minutes
Total conventional marking time		**155 minutes (2h 35m)**

TABLE 21: WCF marking

Task	Time per student	Total time spent
Reading students' work/ note-taking	1 minute per student	30 minutes
Planning a feedback (DIRT) lesson		30 minutes
Total conventional marking time		**60 minutes**

That is a time efficiency saving of around 258 per cent. That is a lot.

What can we learn from this, then, as a leader who establishes what marking and feedback look like in English?

In short: extensive written comments on each student's piece of work is an approach with maximum effort and minimal impact. Conversely, WCF can be viewed as *high-impact, low-effort.*

When we need to manage teacher workload in English, this is an effective tool that genuinely helps.

That said, even with WCF established in your department, there are other things that you can consider that might help to make the marking pressures easier for your department to manage at your school:

Make English the *first* exam in any exam window

I have always managed to ensure this. Obviously, external examinations are scheduled outside of your – or even your school's – control. However, internal examinations and even mock examinations are much easier to time better in order to ensure that your department is not overwhelmed with huge marking loads and short turnaround periods in which to input data.

Every school will have its own policy with regard to data collection or the assessment cycle, to which you will be subject on a whole-school level. However, you need to use your clout as the head of a subject that is double-weighted for Progress 8 and therefore has a hugely significant impact on the school's overall performance at GCSE. Lean into this fact when you speak with your SLT about the timings of things like mock examination windows. It should be relevant if we are going to manage the time pressures to mark English exams that are far greater than in many other (and perhaps all?) other subjects in secondary schools.

The English literature mock exam taking place on 18 November gives your team 24 working days for their marking load. If it takes place on 29 November, it gives them only 15. That is a huge difference for your team and a decision that massively relieves the pressure that they are under during this time of the academic year.

Be selective about what you assess and when

This is something of which to be mindful at Key Stage 3. Consider how your assessment model might create pinch points in your department's time. For example, if units at Key Stage 3 are divided into chunks of time that mirror a half-term or a term, and each one has an end-of-unit assessment, teachers will have a huge influx of marking in the final week of half-term.

You then need to consider the following and the potential impact on staff workload:

- If each assessment includes lengthy essays that need to be marked as well, when are staff given time to complete their marking?
- Do you expect them to do it in half-term?

- When is the deadline to return these assessments to students? Is it reasonable?
- Does this clash with other marking commitments at Key Stage 4 or Key Stage 5?

There are no simple solutions to these but, as an English department lead, you need to always consider how marking might be for a member of your team who teaches 22 out of 25 hours per week and teaches every group, and therefore has a marking load that can feel unsustainable when everything happens all at once.

Possible solutions to ease pressure for your department include:

- using curriculum-related expectations to assess knowledge at a granular level (see Chapter 7) at Key Stage 3 to avoid the burden of essay marking
- staggering when in the term or half-term an assessment takes place – do they always need to take place in the final week of a term, for instance, or could they be staggered (e.g. Year 7, Week 5; Year 8, Week 6; Year 9, Week 7)?
- using comparative judgement (investigate 'no more marking') to assess writing, to reduce the time spent on marking lengthy written tasks.

You might have other creative solutions that would work in your context. As the leader of an English department, you need to always consider how best to support staff with marking and not add unnecessarily to the burden that marking creates.

8. Understand each individual's ways of working

This is something that I became more aware of later in my career, and especially after having children. In order to make your team's lives easier, you need to really know your team – as people and not just as professionals.

I used to work in such a way that I stayed in school until it closed to get my work done, to avoid taking work home. That worked for me *then*. It does not work for me now. I pick up my daughters from nursery each day, so I cannot do what I did in the past. My way of working has shifted because of my home life. I need to manage my workload with this commitment, but as a leader you have to consider and facilitate others in your department to do the same, based on their individual circumstances.

If you have a colleague in your department who has a long commute, do *not* schedule a catch-up, meeting or feedback session before school officially starts simply because that works best for *you*. Consider what works best for them. Cater to their needs where possible. Members of your team might politely smile and agree to such a request, but you might not have considered that it could mean a 5.30 am alarm set in the morning, rather than 6.00 am, because they need to set up their classroom in the morning before school starts.

My advice is to ensure that when you meet with a member of your department, it works on their terms as best as possible. Imagine the difference in response that you will elicit from your colleague in the scenarios below:

- **A:** *Please can we discuss the lesson drop-in tomorrow, first thing? Let's do it before school, as that is probably the best time for it. OK?*
- **B:** *I would love to discuss the lesson drop-in. I appreciate that you have a much longer commute than me, so if tomorrow morning before school doesn't work, let me know. I'll have a look at your timetable and try to find a time that works better.*

Scenario B understands your colleague's way of working better and is more likely to create the conditions for a fruitful discussion than scenario A would. I am not suggesting that you can never meet that colleague in the morning. You are instead acknowledging their context and allowing them to make the choice. They are likely to appreciate this and they are less likely to feel guilty about not being aligned to your way of working. This is important, as you need your team to work in optimal conditions for them.

It will not always be possible to do this for every situation when working with your team, but your awareness of this as a leader will make you a more humane one, which is likely to galvanise your team to work hard towards meeting your vision.

Final thoughts: Empowering your leadership and teaching practice

Something that is often forgotten in leadership positions is the simple fact that you are in the people business. Your colleagues will thrive in their roles if you build the right culture for your team. The best way to do this is by instilling excellent habits and routines for both staff and students on your English corridor. It will lead to the climate of learning necessary for your colleagues to feel empowered, develop their craft and ultimately feel happy and motivated at work every day.

We spend so much of our lives in school, and your job is to ensure that a culture is created for your team where that brings them the professional satisfaction that they crave. Part one of this book demonstrates how you can do this effectively and how this acts as the bedrock for everything that follows. Culture is king.

Whilst no job is perfect, being the leader of a secondary English department is one of the greatest jobs in the world. For me, the opportunity to design a curriculum, shape pedagogy and see the impact of your team's work through assessment is such a satisfying aspect of leading a secondary English department. Hopefully, Part two of this book has inspired some ideas for strengthening your leadership of these three key areas that you need to consider in your role as a leader. I truly believe that if these three areas function in harmony, then it is the recipe for success in securing the best possible outcomes for your students.

The nuts and bolts of leadership in securing these outcomes, though, must not be underestimated. If you have sat through an ineffective department meeting or felt that your head of department placed no value in your professional development – perhaps as a teacher of English earlier in your career – then be better as a leader. Lead CPD from the front, do not get bogged down in admin and always consider how best to develop the skills of your colleagues – the best leaders make those around them better. Remember too what it is like to work a full teaching timetable and consider how to really lighten the load of your team in any way in which you can – even small things make a huge difference. Part three of this book really does offer so many concrete examples of how to do this well, and hopefully there are some things that you can implement tomorrow if you feel inspired.

In writing this book, it really has reminded me of the love that I hold for leading a secondary English department. The impact that you will have as a leader is unfathomable, whether it is the impact on students, parents or colleagues – remember that you are changing lives every single day.

Bibliography

Beck, I., McKeown, M. and Kucan, L. (2013), *Bringing Words to Life: Robust Vocabulary Instruction*, second edition. New York: Guildford Press.
Berger, R. (2003), *An Ethic of Excellence: Building a Culture of Craftsmanship with Students*. Portsmouth, NH: Heinemann.
Boxer, A. (2021), [X] 8 Dec. Available at: https://x.com/adamboxer1/status/1468640276189229064?s=46&t=8aw7L71-2PY90_6OM5WM8w (Accessed: 15 July 2025).
Bruner, J. (1960), *The Process of Education*. Cambridge, MA: The President and Fellows of Harvard College.
Christodoulou, D. (2014), *Seven Myths About Education*. London: Routledge
Clear, J. (2018), *Atomic Habits*. London: Penguin Random House.
Collins, A., Brown, J. S. and Holum, A. (1991), 'Cognitive apprenticeship: Making thinking visible', *American Educator*, 15, (3), 6–11, 38–46.
Counsell, C. (2018), 'Senior curriculum leadership 1: The indirect manifestation of knowledge: (A) curriculum as narrative', *The Dignity of the Thing*, https://thedignityofthethingblog.wordpress.com/2018/04/07/senior-curriculum-leadership-1-the-indirect-manifestation-of-knowledge-a-curriculum-as-narrative
Department for Education (DfE) (2014), National curriculum in England: English programmes of study, www.gov.uk/government/publications/national-curriculum-in-england-english-programmes-of-study/national-curriculum-in-england-english-programmes-of-study
Department for Education (DfE) (2015), National curriculum in England: Science programmes of study, www.gov.uk/government/publications/national-curriculum-in-england-science-programmes-of-study/national-curriculum-in-england-science-programmes-of-study
Department for Education (DfE) (2019), 'Early career framework', www.gov.uk/government/publications/early-career-framework
Department for Education (DfE) (2021a), National curriculum in England: Maths programmes of study, www.gov.uk/government/publications/national-curriculum-in-england-mathematics-programmes-of-study/national-curriculum-in-england-mathematics-programmes-of-study
Department for Education (DfE) (2021b), 'Teachers' Standards: Guidance for school leaders, school staff and governing bodies', https://assets.publish

ing.service.gov.uk/media/61b73d6c8fa8f50384489c9a/Teachers__Standards_Dec_2021.pdf

Didau, D. (2012), 'Slow Writing: how slowing down can improve your writing', *The Learning Spy*, https://learningspy.co.uk/english-gcse/how-to-improve-writing/

Didau, D. (2018), 'Breadth trumps depth', *The Learning Spy*, https://learningspy.co.uk/curriculum/breadth-trumps-depth

Didau, D. (2021a), 'Curriculum related expectations: Using the curriculum as a progression model', *The Learning Spy*, https://learningspy.co.uk/assessment/curriculum-related-expectations

Didau, D. (2021b), *Making Meaning in English: Exploring the Role of Knowledge in the English Curriculum*. Abingdon: Routledge.

du Maurier, D. (1938), 'Chapter one', *Rebecca*. London: Victor Gollancz.

Education Endowment Foundation (EEF) (2021), 'Improving literacy in Key Stage 2: Guidance report', https://educationendowmentfoundation.org.uk/education-evidence/guidance-reports/literacy-ks2

Elliott, V., Baird, J.-A., Hopfenbeck, T. N., Ingram, J., Thompson, I., Usher, N., Zantout, M., Richardson, J. and Coleman, R. (2016), 'A marked improvement? A review of the evidence on written marking', Education Endowment Foundation, https://educationendowmentfoundation.org.uk/education-evidence/evidence-reviews/written-marking

Ericsson, K. A., Krampe, R. T. and Tesch-Römer, C. (1993), 'The role of deliberate practice in the acquisition of expert performance', *Psychological Review*, 100, (3), 363–406.

Ericsson, K.A. and Pool, R. (2016), *Peak: Secrets from the New Science of Expertise*. Boston, MA: Houghton Mifflin Harcourt.

Fordham, M. (2017), 'The curriculum as progression model', *Clio et cetera*, https://clioetcetera.com/2017/03/04/the-curriculum-as-progression-model

Hagger, M. S., Cameron, L. D., Hamilton, K., Hankonen, N. and Linuten, T. (eds) (2020), *The Handbook of Behavior Change*. Cambridge: Cambridge University Press.

Harden, R. M. (1999), 'What is a spiral curriculum?', *Medical Teacher*, 21, (2), 141–143.

Howard, K. (2020), *Stop Talking About Wellbeing: A Pragmatic Approach to Teacher Workload*. Woodbridge: John Catt.

Jerrim, J. and Sims, S. (2019) 'The Teaching and Learning International Survey (TALIS) 2018', Department for Education, https://assets.publishing.service.gov.uk/government/uploads/system/uploads/attachment_data/file/809738/TALIS_2018_research_brief.pdf

Johnston, H. (2012), 'The spiral curriculum: Research into practice', Education Partnerships Inc, https://files.eric.ed.gov/fulltext/ED538282.pdf

Kirby, J. (2023), 'Go upstream', *Joe Kirby*, https://joe-kirby.com/2023/03/25/go-upstream

Lemov, D. (2021), *Teach Like a Champion 3.0: 63 Techniques that Put Students on the Path to College*. Hoboken, NJ: Jossey-Bass.

Lemov, D., Driggs, C. and Woolway, E. (2016), *Reading Reconsidered: A Practical Guide to Rigorous Literacy Instruction*. San Francisco: Jossey-Bass.

Myatt, M. (2018), *The Curriculum: From Gallimaufry to Coherence*. Woodbridge: John Catt.

Myatt, M. (2021), 'Above their pay grade', *Mary Myatt*, www.marymyatt.com/blog/above-their-pay-grade

Myhill, D. (2020), 'Introduction: Rethinking grammar – as choice', https://videnomlaesning.dk/media/3325/27-debra-myhill.pdf

Obama, B. (2008), 'Transcript Of Barack Obama's victory speech', *NPR*, www.npr.org/2008/11/05/96624326/transcript-of-barack-obamas-victory-speech

Ofqual (2018), 'Marking consistency metrics: An update', https://assets.publishing.service.gov.uk/media/5bfbfd70e5274a0fb775cca3/Marking_consistency_metrics_-_an_update_-_FINAL64492.pdf

Ofsted (2015), 'Key Stage 3: The wasted years?', www.gov.uk/government/publications/key-stage-3-the-wasted-years

Ofsted (2019), 'Workbook scrutiny: Ensuring validity and reliability in inspections', https://assets.publishing.service.gov.uk/media/5fb4081de90e0720913b3e11/Inspecting_education_quality_workbook_scrutiny_report.pdf

Ofsted (2021),'Curriculum: Keeping it simple', *Ofsted blog*, https://educationinspection.blog.gov.uk/2021/12/08/curriculum-keeping-it-simple

Ofsted (2024), 'Telling the story: The English education subject report', www.gov.uk/government/publications/subject-report-series-english/telling-the-story-the-english-education-subject-report

Orwell, G. (1945), *Animal Farm*: A Fairy Story, Chapter II.

Pfeffer, J. and Sutton, R.I. (1999), *The Knowing-Doing Gap: How Smart Companies Turn Knowledge into Action*. Boston: Harvard Business School Press.

Pryke, S. and Staniforth, A. (2020), *Ready to Teach: Macbeth: A Compendium of Subject Knowledge, Resources and Pedagogy*. Woodbridge: John Catt Educational.

Quigley, A. (2020), *Closing the Reading Gap*. Abingdon: Routledge.

Rees, T. (2019), 'Helping leaders to keep getting better', Ambition Institute, www.ambition.org.uk/blog/helping-leaders-keep-getting-better

Reynolds, J. (2017), *Long Way Down*. New York: Atheneum.

Rollett, S. (2019), 'Curriculum development: Two key questions', *Stephen Rollett*, https://www.sec-ed.co.uk/content/best-practice/curriculum-development-two-key-questions/

Schleicher, A. (2018), *World Class: How to Build a 21st-Century School System*. Paris: OECD Publishing.

Sealy, C. (2017), 'Memory not memories – teaching for long term learning', *Primarytimerydotcom*, https://primarytimery.com/2017/09/16/memory-not-memories-teaching-for-long-term-learning

Sealy, C. (2020), *The researchED Guide to the Curriculum: An Evidence-Informed Guide for Teachers*. Woodbridge: John Catt Educational.

Sherrington, T. (2018), 'What is a knowledge-rich curriculum? Principle and practice', *teacherhead*, https://teacherhead.com/2018/06/06/what-is-a-knowledge-rich-curriculum-principle-and-practice

Sherrington, T. (2019), 'The #1 problem/weakness in teaching and how to address it', *teacherhead*, https://teacherhead.com/2019/10/04/the-1-problem-weakness-in-teaching-and-how-to-address-it/comment-page-1

Sherrington, T. (2020), 'Teaching for understanding: Schema-building and generative learning', *teacherhead*, https://teacherhead.com/2020/10/04/teaching-for-understanding-schema-building-and-generative-learning

Sherrington, T. (2021), 'The genius of DT Willingham and WDSLS', *teacherhead*, https://teacherhead.com/2021/06/22/the-genius-of-dt-willingham-and-wdsls

Shulman, L. S. (1986), Those who understand: knowledge growth in teaching. Educational Researcher, 15, (2), 4-14.

Teacher Tapp Survey (2024), '*EdTech, Ed (un)Tech, and Progs vs Trads*', UK: January 2024, https://teachertapp.com/uk/articles/edtech-ed-untech-and-progs-vs-trads/

Tomsett, J. (2021), *Cognitive Apprenticeship: In Action*. Woodbridge: John Catt Educational.

Turner, S. (2016), *Secondary Curriculum and Assessment Design*. London: Bloomsbury Education.

Webb, L. (2022), *It's time to talk about teaching motifs* [Twitter thread], July 2022, https://threadreaderapp.com/thread/1550162292326776833

Willingham, D.T. (2010), *Why Students Don't Like School*. San Francisco: Jossey-Bass.

Yousafzai, M. with Lamb, C. (2013), *I Am Malala: The Story of the Girl Who Stood Up for Education and was Shot by the Taliban*. London: Weidenfeld & Nicolson.

Index

Ahmed, Shabnam 50–4
assessment
    assessing pupil progress (APP) 146–7, 149
    assessment foci (AFs) 146–8
    and curriculum-related expectations *see* curriculum-related expectations (CREs)
    and staff workload 232–3
    and Weekly Bulletin 177–9
Atomic Habits (Clear) 51, 52
autonomy 22–4

behaviour management 10–11
    centralised behaviour system 45, 220–2
    consequence 14–15
    removal from class 16
    verbal warning 11–13
bell task 30–1, 40
booklets 45, 201–4, 226
book looks 63–5
    building on previous learning 65–6
    depth and breadth of curriculum coverage 66–7
    practice 68–70
    pupils' progress 67–8

centralised cover booklet 226
centralised resources 200
centrally planned curriculum 45
classroom-based routines 20–1
co-curricular reading programme 113–16
cold-calling 39–42, 53
collaborative planning
    in department meetings 192
    and subject knowledge and expertise 198
common, school-wide language 45
comprehensive resource packs, developing 198–9
consistency 22–4, 26
continuing professional development (CPD) 20, 199–200, 205, 206
    and deliberate practice 57
    leading from the front 209–13
core concepts 83–6
core homework, Key Stage 4 224–5
cover work 225–6
    centralised cover booklet 226
    guided reading 226–7
    knowledge organiser work 226
CPD *see* continuing professional development (CPD)
crossing-out method 131–2
culture
    behaviour of students 11–16
    classroom-based routines 20–1
    consistency vs autonomy 22–4
    CPD 20
    critique 188–9
    and curriculum 17–20
    definition of 5–6
    destination story 7–9
    and mental models 9–10

Index

and teamship 21–2
curriculum 77–9
    and culture 17–20
    golden threads of 86–7, 105–12
    knowledge-rich *see* knowledge-rich curriculum
    spiral *see* spiral curriculum
curriculum designing/ planning
    assessment and ongoing development 96
    case study 92–7
    challenges and lessons learned 96–7
    cohesive curriculum 94–5
    reflections and theories 93
    structured knowledge and skills 96
    texts selection 95–6
    thinking process 79–81
curriculum-related expectations (CREs) 150–5
    assessment 166–9
    grammatical structures 154–5
    progression model 155–62
    purpose of (case study) 165–9
    reporting 162–5
    thesis statement 154

DAFOREST model, of persuasive writing 101–3
deliberate practice 56–61
department meetings 50, 173–4
    culture critique 188–9
    research-linked think piece 179–82
    standardisation and moderation 186–8
    subject knowledge 182–3
    subject-specific pedagogy 183–5
    Weekly Bulletin 174–9
disciplinary knowledge 86–9
'do now' activity 30–1, 46–7, 53
drop-ins 61–3, 188
Dyke, James 44–50

echo reading 114
enhance homework, Key Stage 4 225
exam schedule 232
exam technique 131
    GCSE 131–4
    A level 134–7
excellence building, through routines and habits (case study) 44–50
exit routine 36–7, 216
explicit vocabulary instruction 115

feedback 47–8, 49–50, 227–8
formative assessment 167, 168
four Rs
    recall 71, 72
    replan 72, 73
    reteach 72, 73
    reward 71, 72
framing, and CPD 210–11
Frayer model 137–41

golden threads of curriculum 86–7, 105–12
grammatical structures 154–5
guided reading 226–7

habits *see* routines and habits
habitual learning (case study) 50–4
Handbook of Behavior Change, The (Hagger et al.) 51, 52–3
homework
    centralised homework system 222–5
    core homework 224–5
    enhance homework 225
Hussain, Miriam 197–200

'I do, we do, you do' model 48, 127–30
independent reading 224
'I say, you say' activity 37–9

Johnston, Grace 142–4

knowing–doing gap 56
knowledge and skill 18–19

knowledge organiser work 226
knowledge-rich curriculum 99–101
    breadth and depth 113
    co-curricular reading
        programme 113–16
    golden threads 86–7, 105–12
    persuasive writing 101–5

LEAD principles 180–2
learning walks 61–3
lecture series 204–6
lesson spotlights 61–3
Litdrive 206, 207

marking load 227–33
Massolit, video lectures 207
McNally, Elaine 190–3
meetings *see* department meetings
memory 81
mental models 9–10
metaphors 87–9, 152, 156–8
mindset 40
mini-whiteboards (MWBs) 31–2,
    47, 188–9
    factual recall 34–5
    mental models 35–6
    student behaviour 33
moderation 186, 187–8

'non-example' section, Frayer model
    138, 192

Ofsted 64, 81, 114, 211
online-reading platforms 223
organisation method 216–17

paired academic reading 210
*Peak: Secrets from the New Science of
    Expertise* (Ericsson) 56–7
photocopying 219–20
Pole, Kirsty 165–9
professional development *see*
    continuing professional
    development (CPD)

professional resources, use of 191

quality assurance 55–6

Reading Reconsidered (Lemov et al.) 89
reading reflections, in Weekly
    Bulletin 176
reading with a ruler 114
Recall 6 30–1, 40, 46–7
reflection, significance of 9

removal from class, behaviour
    system 16
replan 72, 73
reporting, of assessment 162–5
research-linked think piece,
    department meeting 179–82
reteach 72, 73
retrieval practice 30–31, 34, 46–47,
    130, 169, 226
'review now' activity 49
Reward, Recall, Reteach, Replan (the
    Four Rs) 71–73
routines and habits 25–6, 43–50, 235
    cold-calling 39–42
    habitual learning (case
        study) 50–4
    'I say, you say' activity 37–9
    meet and greet activity 26–8
    mini-whiteboards 31–6, 47
    recall/retrieval practice 30–
        1, 46–7
    silent entry practice 28–30

sanction escalation system 220–1
schema-building 81–87
self-assessment, student 228, 230
sentence drafting 47
Sherrington, Tom 40, 81, 83, 99,
    106, 176
'show call' activity 49–50
silent entry routine 28–30
skill and knowledge 18–19
spiral curriculum 81–82, 91–92

Staniforth, Amy 92–7
student accountability 48
student feedback 62–63
subject knowledge 182–3, 195–7
    audit 182, 204
    booklets 201–4
    case studies 197–200, 209–13
    CPD videos 206–7
    lecture series 204–6
    walking talking mocks (for staff) 208–9
subject-specific pedagogy
    consistency (case study) 142–4
    and department meeting 183–5
    exam technique 131–7
    introduction writing 120–3
    live modelling 125–30
    metaphors 123–5
    structures 117–23
    vocabulary instruction 137–42

Teach Like a Champion (Lemov) 26
teamship 21–2, 174, 191
tenor 87, 89, 154, 175
terminology 49
Theory of Planned Behaviour 53

thesis statements 154, 175
'turn, talk, write, feedback' approach 47–8

vehicle 87, 89, 154, 175
verbal paraphrasing of answers, avoiding 42–3
verbal warning 11–13
vocabulary drilling 47
vocabulary instruction, explicit 89–91

walking talking mocks (WTMs) 208–9
Weekly Bulletin
    assessment and data 177–9
    curriculum 176–7
    key reminders 174
    meetings and deadlines 174
    news and updates 174
    reading reflections 176
    staff shout-out 174
    teaching and learning 175
whole-class feedback 50, 227–8, 229, 231
'Why that method?' sheets 143–4
word web 91
Wright, Heather 209–13